13-Week Devotional

MOSES
AND
JESUS
AND
ME!

Discovering Jesus in the
Old Testament Stories of Moses

FOR GIRLS AGES 6–9

HENDRICKSON
PUBLISHERS

ROSE
KiDZ

Moses and Jesus and Me!

Cover design by Emily Heintz
Interior design by Drew McCall
Written by Mary Gross Davis

Unless otherwise indicated, all Scripture quotations are taken from the Holy
Bible, New Living Translation, copyright © 1996, 2004, 2015 by Tyndale
House Foundation. Used by permission of Tyndale House Publishers, Inc.,
Carol Stream, Illinois 60188. All rights reserved.

Scripture quotations marked (NIrv) are taken from the Holy Bible, New
International Reader's Version®, NIrv ® Copyright © 1995, 1996, 1998,
2014 by Biblica, Inc.™ Used by permission of Zondervan. All rights reserved
worldwide. www.zondervan.com The "NIrv" and "New International
Reader's Version" are trademarks registered in the United States Patent and
Trademark Office by Biblica, Inc.™

ISBN: 978-1-62862-814-2
RoseKidz® reorder# L50036
Juvenile Nonfiction/Religion/ Devotion & Prayer

Printed in United States of America
Printed December 2018

CONTENTS

INTRODUCTION

Name a superhero? That's easy! There are so many!

Superheroes are strong. They can save people. They can do amazing things! They are really cool.

But has a superhero ever saved YOU? No? Why not? They're not real? Not even WONDER WOMAN?

You're right! Unless . . .You look in the Bible. What? Yes! In the Bible!

We're going to meet a real hero, Moses. He helped to save millions of people! But God told Moses this promise:

> "I will raise up a prophet like you [Moses] from among their fellow Israelites. I will put my words in his mouth, and he will tell the people everything I command him."
>
> Deuteronomy 18:18

You mean there is an even BETTER hero than Moses? Who was God talking about? Who has saved more people than Moses? Done more amazing things?

You guessed it! JESUS! He is real. And he can do anything.

Let's find out more about Moses and Jesus, and YOU!

ACTiViTY SUPPLY LiST

Many activities in this devotional require supplies. Some are reoccurring and are listed under the Basic Craft Materials list or the Basic Kitchen Materials list. These should be on hand at all times. Other materials that may not be readily available in your house are listed under the "additional materials" lists for specific weeks. Consider looking ahead a week or two so you are prepared for the activities as they arise.

Basic Craft Materials

- ruler
- scissors
- glue
- tape
- colored paper
- white paper
- permanent markers
- markers
- pencils
- index cards
- butcher paper
- paper plates
- yarn

Basic Kitchen Materials

- plastic wrap
- mixing bowl
- large spoon
- silverware
- measuring spoons
- water
- ice
- sugar
- salt
- vanilla extract

Additional Materials for Week 1

- brown paper or other heavy paper

Additional Materials for Week 2

- marshmallows
- stick of butter
- cinnamon
- crescent roll dough
- stamp or ink pad

Additional Materials for Week 4

- gumdrops or mini marshmallows
- toothpicks

Additional Materials for Week 5

- cornstarch
- fruit flavored, sugar-free gelatin
- gallon- and quart-sized resealable freezer bags
- half-and-half
- rock salt or ice-cream salt
- smooth rocks

Additional Materials for Week 6

- clear glass
- red food coloring
- bleach
- basketball and goal

Additional Materials for Week 7

- wide-mouthed glass container
- mirror small enough to fit into the container
- flashlight

Additional Materials for Week 8

- envelope of baker's yeast
- clean, clear bottle with narrow neck
- balloon or rubber glove
- empty paper-towel or toilet-paper tubes
- cups
- marbles
- 9x13-inch baking pan
- all-purpose flour
- baking soda
- unsweetened cocoa powder
- vegetable oil
- white vinegar
- chocolate chips
- baking parchment (optional)

Additional Materials for Week 9

- blindfold

Additional Materials for Week 10

- cube-shaped box of any size
- beach ball or playground ball
- stickers (optional)

Additional Materials for Week 11

- watercolor markers
- styrofoam plates or trays
- paintbrush (optional)

Additional Materials for Week 12

- oil pastels
- pipe cleaners
- pony beads
- wooden beads
- plastic straws
- clear Con-Tact paper (optional)

Additional Materials for Week 13

- craft foam square
- cardboard square the same size as the craft foam
- metal brad
- large paper clip
- latex or rubber gloves
- trash bags

Optional

- recycled materials (egg carton, soda bottle, soup can, etc.)
- modeling clay
- bread (sturdy bread like multigrain works best)
- nut butter
- bananas, berries, nuts, cereal pieces, etc.

"For I know the plans I have for you," says the Lord.
"They are plans . . . to give you a future and hope."

Jeremiah 29:11

PLANNED BY GOD

SAVED BY A BABY

EXODUS 1:1—2:10; MATTHEW 1:18-25

Pharaoh was the king of Egypt. And Pharaoh had a problem. Long ago, a big family had settled in his land. This family became very big. There were millions of them.

They were called the Israelites. They were God's chosen people. And they were very sad. You see, the king made them his slaves. They worked very hard for no pay.

They began to ask God for help. God had a plan. And God's plan was a baby.

A BABY?

Pharaoh wanted to get rid of every Israelite baby boy when Moses was born. But one family hid their new baby brother. How long could they hide him? What could they do?

God had a plan. He gave the mother a good idea. She covered a basket in tar so it floated. She put her baby inside and took the basket boat to the river.

The baby's big sister, Miriam, stayed to watch the basket boat. Soon, the princess came to the river. She was the Pharaoh's daughter! She saw the little floating basket boat.

She had a servant bring it to her. They opened the basket— inside was a crying BABY!

"Oh, it's an Israelite baby!" said the princess. "Isn't he cute? He must be hungry."

Just then, Miriam stepped up. She said, "Do you need someone to feed this hungry baby? I know just the person."

"Yes, go get the person you have in mind," said the princess.

Miriam brought her mother. The princess paid Miriam's mother to care for her own baby. The princess also named this baby. She called him Moses.

"His name means, 'lifted out.' Because he was in the water and I lifted him out," said the princess.

When he was older, Moses lived at Pharaoh's palace as the princess's son. Moses was lifted out of danger. He was lifted out of being a slave. He became a prince.

God had a plan. This baby was part of God's plan to help those sad Israelites. That's amazing!

But years later, God had an even greater plan. God's even greater plan was another baby.

An angel said, "Call this baby Jesus, because he will save his people from their sins." Jesus is God's own Son. Jesus was the baby God sent.

He was born to fulfill God's biggest plan—to save the whole world! That's even greater! God had a great plan for Moses. God had a greater plan for Jesus. And it's good to know that God has a great plan for you, too!

YOUR TURN

For each question below, write your answer
in the word bubble of the same color.

What was God's big plan for Moses?

How did
God save
Moses' life?

What big plan
did God have
for Jesus?

FAMiLY MATCH UP

Moses grew up with a mismatched family identity. He didn't find out that he was an Israelite until he was grown-up. In this game, your family will get all mixed up. You'll have to match them back together. This game can be played alone or with other people.

1. Write each family member's name on two index cards. Include cousins, grandparents, aunts, and uncles, too. The more the better!

2. Shuffle the cards.

3. Place each card face down on the table.

4. Flip two cards over at a time. If they match you get to keep them! If they don't, turn them over.

5. When you find a match, share a memory about that person. If you're playing by yourself, write your memory in a journal, or say a quick prayer for that person.

Tip: Try to remember which ones you turn over so that you can find matches better.

Bonus Fun: Interview Your Family

Find an older person in your family. Ask that person to tell you about a time when God helped them know what to do. For more fun, ask a family member to record the story!

How would you respond if someone asked you about a time God helped you?

PRAYER

God has good plans for you!
What are things you may do when you are bigger? Write words or draw pictures here. Then ask God what he wants you to know about his plans for you. Then, listen!

GET OUT GRACEFULLY

Lia ballerina is all mixed up! She needs to get through the maze. Pick up each word of Jeremiah 29:11 in the correct path of the maze and write them on the lines below.

"_____ _____ _____ _____

_____ _____ _____ _____

_____," _____ _____ _____.

"_____ _____ _____

... _____ _____ _____ ____

_____ _____ ____ _____."

Jeremiah 29:11

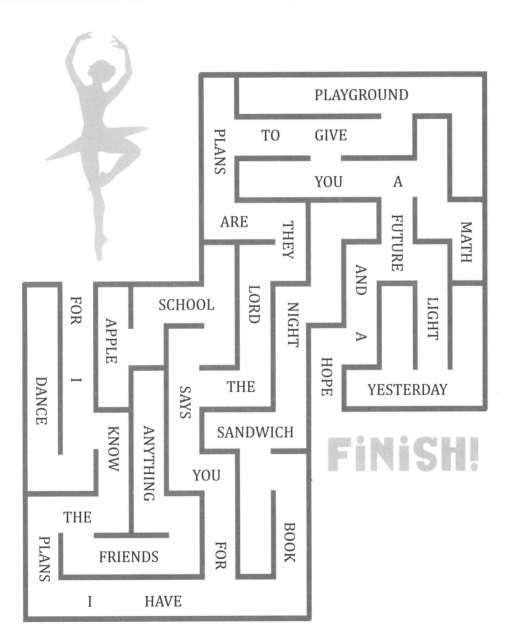

PLAYGROUND

PLANS   TO   GIVE

YOU   A

ARE   THEY   FUTURE   MATH

FOR   SCHOOL   LORD   NIGHT   AND   A   LIGHT

APPLE   THE   HOPE   YESTERDAY

DANCE   I   SAYS   FINISH!

KNOW   ANYTHING   SANDWICH

YOU

THE   BOOK

PLANS   FRIENDS   FOR

I   HAVE

Answers on Page 220

GOD KNOWS MY NAME

Hannah never thought about her name. She could write it. She answered when someone called, "Hannah!" She even knew that her name was the same backwards as forwards. But she never wondered what it meant.

One day, Hannah and Grandma were making cookies together.

Grandma asked, "Did you know that you're named after your great-great-grandma? Her name was Hannah, too. She had lots of adventures with God!"

Hannah was busy pushing cookie dough onto the cookie sheet. She asked, "Why was I named for great-great-grandma Hannah?"

Grandma said, "I think it was because of what her name means. It means 'grace.'"

"Like a graceful ballerina?" asked Hannah.

"Not exactly," said Grandma. "Grace is more like the kindness of God. Your parents felt that God showed kindness to them when you were born. And they remembered how much Grandma Hannah loved God. They wanted you to be like her!"

"They could have named me after you, Grandma."

Grandma laughed. "I guess they could have, but my name just means flower. I think they wanted you to think bigger. They wanted you to know how kind God is—from your name and from everything else he does for you!"

Grandma went on, "Just think of the ways God is kind to you—every day! You wake up in the morning because God is kind. You have a warm bed and food for breakfast because God is kind. The sun, the rain . . ."

"I guess everything is because God is kind!" laughed Hannah.

"Yes!" said Grandma. She pulled a sheet of cookies from the oven. "Even cookies are because God is kind!"

"God knows our names," Grandma went on. "He is kind to all of us! And he's got a plan for each of us. That's how we have adventures in God's story—by listening to him and obeying. Just like Great-Great-Grandma Hannah did!"

YOUR TURN

What's in My Name?

Do you know what your name means? If you don't, ask a family member to help you find the meaning of your name. Write it on the lines below. Then, in the space on the next page, write your name BIG. Decorate it with colored pencils!

_____

_____

_____

_____

_____

_____

_____

_____

_____

FAMILY QUILT

Names can link families together across generations. Everyone's family is different. Some people have many siblings and some have none. Some live with grandparents and some are adopted. The people in your family impact your life every day. You are woven together like the threads of a quilt. Make your own family quilt to show who makes up your family.

What You'll Need

- brown paper or other heavy paper
- ruler
- pencils
- scissors
- butcher paper
- markers
- glue
- tape

What You'll Do

1. Use a ruler and pencil to draw a grid on butcher paper, with 8x8–inch squares. This will be your quilt template. Make sure there is at least one square in the grid for each family member.

2. Cut brown paper or other heavy paper into 8x8–inch squares, making at least one for each family member.

3. Each person designs and colors their own quilt square or squares. Doodle, decorate, draw pictures of things you like or write words about God's plan in your life.

4. Make more than one square if you have time and ideas! If you have pets, make squares for them, too!

5. Lay out the finished squares on your template (from step 1). Move them around to see what arrangement looks best.

6. Glue finished squares onto the butcher paper grid to make a family quilt. Display the paper quilt by taping it to a wall. Talk about how each family member decorated their squares. Find out the stories behind each person's decorations!

PLAN A TRiP!

Many places around the world are named after famous people. The Philippines are named after King Philip of Spain. Colombia is named after Christopher Columbus. If you could name a country after yourself, what would you call it? Write it on the line below.

_____

What would your country look like? Is it beachy or snowy? Draw a picture below.

If someone were planning a trip to your country, what would they need to bring? Make a list below.

_____

_____

_____

Bonus Fun

Spending time with family is extra fun when you're on vacation. But you don't have to wait for summer to plan a trip. You don't have to GO anywhere to plan a trip! You can do this with your family, or with a friend, or by yourself! Choose a place you would like to go—anywhere! Find a map of that place. (Libraries have big maps. Or print out an online map.) Find out how far that place is from where you live.

- Make a list of the things you would take with you.

- Make a list of fun things to see near that place.

You could even make a plan for how you would travel to that place!

PRAYER

Dear God, I am glad that you know my name. I am glad you have a plan for my life. Thank you for helping me know the best way to live. In Jesus' name, amen.

*God is our refuge and strength, always
ready to help in times of trouble.*

Psalm 46:1

PROTECTED BY GOD

RUN FROM DANGER

EXODUS 2:11-25; MATTHEW 2:13-23

Moses grew to a man. He lived like a prince! He wore fancy Egyptian clothes. Servants did what he wanted. But still, Moses knew he was an Israelite. And the Israelites were slaves. Moses wanted to help his people.

One day, Moses was watching some Israelites work. He saw an Egyptian slave master hurting an Israelite slave— and Moses decided that he would save the Israelite.

Moses attacked the Egyptian. The Egyptian died! Moses dug a hole in the sand and buried him. He thought no one saw him do this terrible thing.

But the very next day, Moses saw two Israelites fighting. He asked, "Why are you hurting each other?"

One man said, "Who are you to tell us what to do? You killed the Egyptian. Are you going to kill me, too?"

Suddenly, Moses was scared. And then, he heard that the king was looking for him—to kill him! Moses was in big trouble.

Moses ran away from Egypt. But God knew where he was. God was protecting him. Even though he had done wrong, God loved Moses and had a plan for his life!

Finally, Moses came to a far place. *Surely no one would find me here*, he thought. He met a family whose father invited Moses to stay with them. For years, Moses hid, caring for the family's sheep. He even married one of the family's daughters. Moses and his wife had two sons.

All this time, God was protecting Moses—and Moses didn't even know it! Remember how God had a plan to help the Israelites? Well, God had a plan for Moses. It was a great plan to make Moses a great leader and save lots of people's lives! What could be greater than that?

Thousands of years later, Jesus was in the same position. King Herod wanted to kill him—and he was only a little kid! But God spoke to Jesus' earthly father, Joseph, in a dream. God told Joseph "Get up NOW and take Jesus and Mary, all the way to Egypt!" And Joseph did. The family hid in Egypt until God sent an angel to tell Joseph it was safe to come back!

God protected Moses because he had a great plan for Moses. But God had an even greater plan for Jesus—and God protected him when he was little. And here is something good to know: God has a plan for you, too! You don't need to worry or be afraid. God will protect you and show you what to do!

YOUR TURN

For each question below, write your answer in the word bubble of the same color.

Why did Moses run away?

What's a time when you might want to run away?

Why did Jesus' family run away?

What can you remember about God in scary times?

29

HIDEOUT

When Moses and Jesus ran away, they looked for a safe place to hide. Pretend you are a superhero and build a safety fort for yourself. Use pillows, sheets, and blankets to make it cozy. You can even use clothespins and string to hold up the sheets!

Bonus Fun

Important things should be saved in special places.

1. Take some of your favorite toys and hide them around the house.

2. Write down where you hid them so you don't forget.

3. Invite a parent or sibling to find them. As they get closer to the hidden object, say "warmer." As they get farther from the hidden object, say "colder."

PRAYER

Draw a picture of a hiding place. How is God
like a safe place to hide? While you draw, pray
and thank God for being your protector.

MEMORY VERSE SCRAMBLE

Sometimes things hide in plain sight and we still miss them. In this game, you'll have to be extra sharp to put the hidden message back together.

What You'll Need

- brown paper or other heavy paper
- ruler

What You'll Do

1. Write each word of the Bible verse on its own index card. Write the reference on a card, too!

2. Mix up the cards.

3. Drop them around the room. Or just throw them up and let them fly!

4. Call out, "Scramble!" Everyone grabs at least one card.

Note: You can play this game by yourself, but it's even more fun with other family members or friends.

See how quickly you can put the words in order! Read the verse aloud together. Then try it again—can you do it faster?

God is our refuge
and strength, always
ready to help in
times of trouble.

Psalm 46:1

33

WHAT'S THAT SOUND?

Bumpa thumpa bumpa thumpa bumpa thumpa! The noise was loud. Julisa pulled the covers up in bed. *What was that?* she wondered. Her heart was beating fast.

She looked out the window. It wasn't thunder. It wasn't raining. It wasn't the wind. There was only a tiny breeze.

Then, it happened again—*bumpa thumpa bumpa thumpa bumpa thumpa.* Julisa wanted to jump up and run to her parents' room. But she felt like she could not move. She felt frozen!

Julisa squeezed her eyes shut. "Dear God," she said, "I am scared. Help!"

Just then she remembered some Bible words she had memorized: "In peace I will lie down and sleep, for you alone, O LORD, will keep me safe," (Psalm 4:8).

Julisa took a deep breath. She felt less scared. In a little while, she even fell back to sleep!

The next morning, Dad asked Julisa, "Did you hear old Rory on the roof last night?"

"What? Who's Rory?" asked Julisa.

"Rory is a big old raccoon. He walks across the roof almost every night. He usually wakes Mom and me with his big *bumpa thumpa bumpa thumpa* noise. But last night, he kept walking—right over your room!"

Julisa's eyes got big. "Really? It was a raccoon? I was so scared!"

"If you were scared, why didn't you come to us?" asked Mom.

"Mom! I couldn't move! I was frozen!" said Julisa.

"That's OK," said Dad. "When people get scared, sometimes they run. But sometimes, they sit very still. What else did you do?"

"I prayed. Then I remembered Bible words about God keeping me safe," said Julisa.

"That's great! God answered your prayer with that Bible verse! Good job!" said Mom. "And thank you, God! You kept Julisa safe—even though Rory isn't very scary when you get to know him. Just noisy!"

YOUR TURN

Can you imagine if you had a zoo on your roof? What would the animals sound like? Raccoons make a scratchy sound with their grippy feet. Horses would make a clicky sound with their hooves. Elephants would make a booming sound. Animal footprints are all different. In the space provided, make your own fingerprint critters.

What You'll Need

- stamp pad
- markers or pencils

What You'll do

1. Press your finger on a stamp pad, and then onto the page on the right.

2. Use a marker or pencil to make legs, eyes, and other parts.

SHAKE UP SALT

We react to sounds around us all day. In the morning, an alarm wakes us up. At the end of a school day, the bell tells us we're free! Usually, sounds make us move. But with this experiment you can SEE sounds move.

What You'll Need

- plastic wrap

- mixing bowl

- salt

- large spoon

What You'll Do

1. Pull off enough plastic wrap from the roll to cover the top of the mixing bowl.

2. With the help of a grown-up, stretch the wrap over the top of the bowl so that it stays tight and smooth.

3. Sprinkle salt over the plastic wrap.

4. Now tap the side of the mixing bowl to make sound.

What do you see? What happens to the salt?
Sound waves make the salt dance!

PRAYER

Dear God, thank you for protecting me. When I am afraid, help me remember to trust you and ask you what to do. In Jesus' name, amen.

HiDeOUTS!

This recipe is simple and fun to make. The marshmallows disappear once you cook the dough leaving a "cave" in the middle! While you work, talk about how God is like a hiding place. Tell stories about ways he has helped you and your family.

What You'll Need

- 16 marshmallows

- ½ cup (1 stick) butter, melted

- ¼ cup sugar

- 2 tablespoons cinnamon

- 2 (8-ounce) cans of crescent-roll dough

What You'll Do

1. Mix sugar and cinnamon in a small bowl.

2. On a baking sheet, unroll crescent-roll dough. Separate each roll along the dotted lines.

3. Roll marshmallows in melted butter, and then in cinnamon-sugar mixture. Tip: To avoid messy hands, skewer the marshmallow on a corn holder.

4. Set a coated marshmallow in the middle of an unrolled crescent dough segment.

5. Roll the dough around the marshmallow until it is completely covered. Push in the sides as you go.

6. Pinch seams on either end to seal each roll. Make sure the marshmallow is completely covered by the dough. If not, the marshmallow will seep out while baking.

7. Place rolls on a baking sheet, and bake at 375°F for about 12 minutes.

8. After removing rolls from the oven, brush with remaining melted butter and then sprinkle with remaining cinnamon-sugar mixture. Serve warm.

We are God's masterpiece. He has created us anew in Christ Jesus, so we can do the good things he planned for us long ago.

Ephesians 2:10

CALLED BY GOD

BURNING BUSH

EXODUS 3:1–4:31; MATTHEW 3:13–16

Moses had lived far from Egypt for years and years. But God hadn't forgotten his plan for Moses and for his people!

Moses was a shepherd. It was hard, hot work. But one day, Moses followed a wandering sheep. He saw a bush on fire— but it wasn't burning up! Moses went over to see it.

He heard a voice call, "Moses! Moses!" It was God's voice!

Moses knew it was God. "Yes, Lord." Moses answered.

"Take off your shoes," said God. "You are standing on holy ground." Moses took off his shoes. *What does GOD want from me?* Moses must have wondered.

"Moses," God said, "I want you to lead my people away from Pharaoh and Egypt. Lead them to a new home. I will show you where to go."

But Moses didn't want to go back to Egypt! He said, "What if people don't believe you sent me?"

God told Moses, "I'll make sure people believe you. Watch. Throw your walking stick onto the ground." Moses did—and it became a snake! Yes, God could do that!

Then God told Moses to pick up the snake by the tail. It turned back into his stick!

God told him to put his hand into his robe and pull it out. Moses did. Eewww! His hand had a horrible disease.

Then God told Moses put his hand back into his robe. He pulled it out again—his hand was fine! God proved he can do anything! He proved that he could help Moses.

But Moses still said, "Lord, please send someone else to do it! I'm not good at speaking in front of crowds."

God reminded Moses, "I made your mouth. I know you. And I will help you! I will be with you."

But God understood Moses's fear so he said, "Your brother Aaron can speak well. I will tell you what to say. You can tell Aaron. He can speak to the people. Take your walking stick. Remember, I will help you do those amazing things!"

God had called Moses to do an important job. He even sent Aaron way out into the desert to meet Moses. There, Moses told Aaron everything.

Then, Moses and Aaron did go back to Egypt! They called the Israelite leaders together. They told them that God had heard their prayers. God was going to get them out of Egypt!

God had a big job for Moses to do. But he didn't have to do it alone. He had God's help!

Thousands of years later, God called Jesus to save the whole world! When Jesus was baptized, God sent his Holy Spirit like a dove. It rested on Jesus. God said, "This is my dearly loved Son, who brings me great joy (Matthew 3:17)!"

God showed Moses he would give Moses the power he needed to do a great thing. God showed Jesus he would give Jesus all the power he needed to do the world's greatest job.

God has an important job for you, too! You don't have to wait until you are a grown-up. Look for the ways God is getting you ready right now. God has great things for you to do in his kingdom!

YOUR TURN

For each question below, write your answer in the word bubble of the same color.

How did God appear to Moses?

How did God comfort Moses?

How did God show he had chosen Jesus?

FiRe MAZe

God spoke to Moses in a burning bush. This fire
maze has some words, too. Follow the missing words
from the Bible verse. Then, fill in the blanks.

We are God's _____.

He has created us _____ in

Christ _____,

so we _____

do the _____

things he planned for _____ long ago.

Ephesians 2:10

Answers on Page 220

START

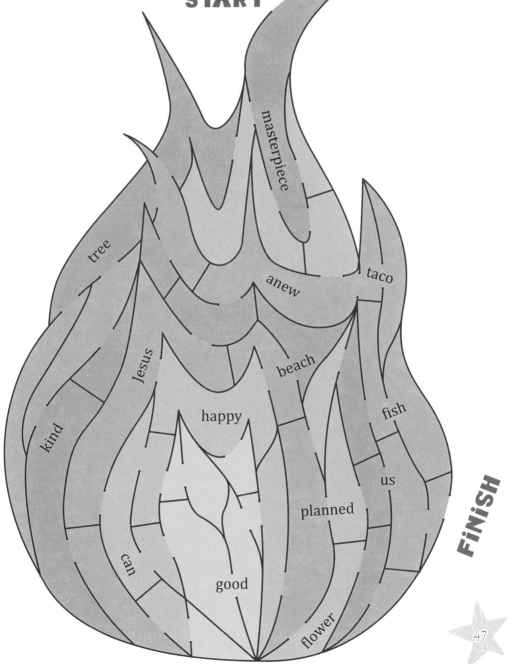

masterpiece

tree

taco

anew

Jesus

beach

kind

happy

fish

us

can

planned

good

flower

FiNiSH

47

A "ME" CHALLENGE

God knows us better than we know ourselves. God says we are his "masterpiece" (Ephesians 2:10)! Genesis tells us he created us with his words. So here is today's challenge: Use your words to describe yourself!

I dream about _____.

I worry about _____.

I am happy when _____.

I am good at _____.

I don't like to _____.

I feel brave when _____.

I am glad that _____.

I would like to be _____ someday.

PRAYER

Because God made you, he knows what jobs you'll be good at. What is a job God might have for you to do right now? A job you might do later?

Draw a picture of yourself doing one of these jobs. Ask God to help you know more about good things you can do right now.

ADDIE'S JOB

Addie's mom and brother were excited! They were packing to go to Nicaragua for two weeks. They were going to help sick people. But Addie was too little to go. She was staying home with Dad and Grandma.

At church, Pastor Jamie called Addie's family to the front. People wanted to pray for Addie's mom and brother before their trip.

Addie felt kind of sad. *I'm not going anywhere,* she thought. *I'm not important.* She looked at the ground. A few tears slid down her cheeks.

When everyone was finished praying, Addie saw her teacher. Miss Grace smiled at Addie and got down on one knee. She waved for Addie to come close.

"Are you feeling left out?" Miss Grace asked. Addie nodded.

"Addie, did you know that God has an important job for you, too?"

Addie was surprised. She said, "I'm just a kid. I'm not important."

"Important? Oh, yes you are!" smiled Miss Grace. "God says you are very important. And he has important things for you to do."

"Like what?" asked Addie.

"Like at church next Sunday. A new girl will be coming to our class. Her name is Jessie. She needs a Class Buddy. Would you be Jessie's Class Buddy?" asked Miss Grace.

"Sure!" said Addie. "That will be fun!"

"It is very important work!" said Miss Grace. "Everyone needs to feel welcomed. You are good at welcoming people, Addie. I think you will do a good job! Thank you, Addie!"

YOUR TURN

Answer the questions about yourself in the spaces provided.

What is something you
are too young to do?

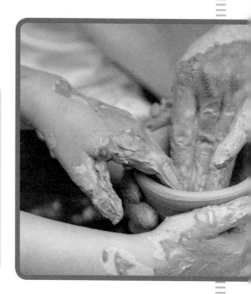

What is something you
are too old to do?

Name two things you
are good at right now.

RACE TO THE CASTLE

Yesterday, Addie felt left out because her family members went on a mission trip. But the great thing about God's royal family is that you are never alone or lost. Pretend you are a princess who needs to get to her castle. Beginning at "Start," draw a line through each word of Ephesians 2:10 in order to find your way home.

We are God's masterpiece.
He has created us anew
in Christ Jesus, so we
can do the good things he
planned for us long ago.

Ephesians 2:10

START

we

masterpiece

He

are God's

has

anew us

created

in

Jesus

do

so

the can

good

we

things

planned

he

for

us

long

ago

FINISH

Answers on Page 220

TALK ABOUT WORK!

The best kind of games include your whole family—that way no one feels left out.

1. Find a paper tube or a toy microphone.

2. Gather your family into one room.

3. Then, use your pretend microphone to play Talk Show!

4. Invite a grown-up in your family to answer questions about their work.

You might ask:

- "What kinds of jobs have you done?"

- "What do you like about your work now?"

- "What is hard about your work?"

- "If you could ask God one question about your work, what would you ask him?"

- "Tell us how God showed you he wanted you to do this job."

- "What would you tell a kid about the work God has for them?"

Grandparents and other older family members are good at this. They have had more jobs!

Bonus Fun

Enlist a sibling or other family member to be your "camera operator" and video the interview or post live on social media.

PRAYER

Dear God, thank you for loving me. Thank you that you have good things planned for me to do. When you talk to me, please help me to listen. I love you! In Jesus' name, amen.

Don't be afraid, for I am with you. Don't discouraged,
for I am your God. I will strengthen you and help you.
I will hold you up with my victorious right hand.

Isaiah 41:10

MADE STRONG BY GOD

LET MY PEOPLE GO

EXODUS 5:1—6:10; MATTHEW 4:17,23-25; JOHN 5:19-21

Moses and his brother Aaron traveled to Egypt. They'd
talked with the Israelite leaders. But now it was time
to talk to Pharaoh. Sure, God had promised to help
Moses. But Moses still did not want to talk to Pharaoh!
Pharaoh was not going to like what Moses said.

Aaron was probably scared, too. This was hard. But
God said to do it. And God said he would help them.

They marched into the palace—where Moses had
once lived! Moses told Pharaoh, "God wants you to let
the Israelite people go so they can worship him."

Pharaoh was mad! "No!" Pharaoh yelled. "I don't know your God. I will not let them go!"

Instead, Pharaoh decided to punish the Israelites. He said, "They want to leave because they're lazy. Make them work harder!"

Pharaoh told his slave masters to make the Israelites gather straw for the bricks. That was more work. But they would have to make the same number of bricks as before! No matter how hard they worked, they could not make the same number of bricks! So Pharaoh's men hurt them!

Now even the Israelites were mad at Moses. "This is your fault," they said. "Since you came, things are even worse!"

Nothing seemed to be going the way Moses expected. What could Moses do? Moses prayed to God. God told him, "I will show my power. Pharaoh will let the Israelites go. I promised to give my people a new home. I will rescue them from slavery in Egypt.

"Now you go back and tell Pharaoh again: 'Let my people go!'"

Wow. Moses and Aaron needed to obey, and to trust God. It did not look like anything good was happening. But, even when it was hard, they had to believe that God would help them. So they trusted God. And soon, God did help them. Moses and Aaron had great faith. But Jesus' faith was greater!

Like Moses, Jesus often talked to people who were angry at him. But Jesus still talked to them. He obeyed God—always. Every day, he listened to God. He found out what God wanted him to do. Then Jesus did it. Even when it was very hard, Jesus obeyed.

He knew God his Father would keep his promises. By fully obeying God, Jesus showed he is God's perfect Son. And he obeyed—even when obeying meant he had to die. Because he died, we can join God's family! That's the greatest thing ever! It's greater than anything Moses did!

And it's good to know that God will help you, even when people are mean. He will help you to trust him even when it seems like nothing good is happening!

YOUR TURN

For each question below, write your answer in the word bubble of the same color.

Who was NOT glad to hear from Moses?

Who blamed Moses that they had to work harder?

What did Moses do when things were not easy?

What does God want you to do when things are hard? When people are mean?

61

A STRONG HAND!

Have you ever arm wrestled someone? Some people will not let go. Even when it's clear the other person is stronger. God was stronger than Pharaoh, but Pharaoh would not let the Israelites go. Test your arm strength with these challenges

Cut a lemon in half. Which hand can squeeze more juice out of a lemon half?

Take a pencil and paper. Which hand can write your name neater?

Take a tennis ball outdoors. Using only one hand, which hand can bounce it on the ground and catch it more times?

Most people are right-handed. That is why God says he will hold you up with his right hand! God's is the strongest hand ever!

PRAYER

Dear God,

I don't feel strong when _____.

I feel afraid when _____.

Thank you that you promise to help me be strong when I feel weak. Thank you for your promise to help me when I am afraid. In Jesus' name, amen.

STRONG SHAPES!

Certain shapes are stronger than others. The triangle is the strongest shape in the world. Look at the Egyptian pyramids! They have lasted hundreds of years—through sandstorms and desert heat—because of their shape.

Look at the pyramid below. How many triangles can you find? Hint: Some triangles are inside others.

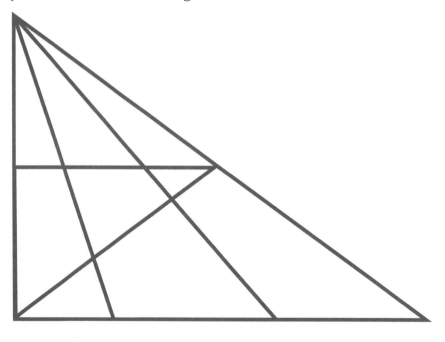

Answers on Page 221

Bonus Fun

Build your own pyramid with this fun activity. Try different shapes, too.

What You'll Need

- gum drops or mini marshmallows

- toothpicks

- paper plates

What You'll Do

1. Put some gum drops on one plate, and use another plate as the base for your building.

2. Push the toothpicks into the gum drops gently to make a building. Does it work better to make a building out of squares? Out of triangles? Can you build a bridge?

BiKiNG BRAVeRY

Ellie loved to ride her bike! All morning, she had ridden up and down the block. Daddy had told her not to go past the corner. So she would ride up to the corner and then turn around.

But at noon, Daddy came home for lunch. Ellie said, "Daddy, I want to ride farther. May I ride to Aunt Libby's house this afternoon?" Aunt Libby's house was six blocks away.

Daddy smiled. "Do you feel scared to go so far alone?"

"Kind of," said Ellie. "But maybe you could go with me!"

"Good idea," said Daddy. "When we finish lunch, you can ride to Aunt Libby's. I'll follow you in my truck."

Ellie ate as fast as she could! Then she got out her bike. Her dad

got into his truck. All the way to Aunt Libby's house, her dad drove slowly and stayed close to Ellie.

When Ellie saw Aunt Libby's tiny green house, she smiled. *Almost there*, she thought. Ellie gripped her handles extra tight and peddled hard. She heard Daddy's motor grumble louder. He was trying to keep up with her.

Ellie parked her bike near the front door. She waited for Daddy to get out of his truck. Both Daddy and Ellie knocked on Aunt Libby's door.

She opened the door and smiled! "I'm glad to see you, Ellie!" she said. "You rode your bike here?"

Ellie smiled back. She said, "Yes! Daddy said I could! And he was with me all the way!"

Aunt Libby laughed. "I know just what you mean! God is my Heavenly Daddy. When he says I can do something, he helps me to do it. And he is always with me, too!"

Daddy laughed. "That's true!" he said.

Daddy gave Ellie a hug. "I have to get back to work. Call Mama before you leave here. Tell her you will ride home. And tell her I said you could do it!"

YOUR TURN

Draw or write your answers:

1. What rules are hard to obey?

2. What things are hard to wait for?

3. What is something God says you can do?

1.

2.

3.

69

I CAN SEE CLEARLY!

Sometimes it's scary or unsafe to go places by yourself. You might catch a shadow from the corner of your eye and think it's something bad. Then you find out it's a rabbit. Shadows are tricky things! Today, go outside for a Shadow Walk.

1. Take some paper and a pencil with you. Don't try this at noon. There won't be many shadows.

2. Look around your yard or your neighborhood. Where do you see shadows? Can you tell what is making the shadow?

3. Now, put your paper behind the item so that the shadow is cast on your paper.

4. Use your pencil to draw around the shape of the shadow.

5. Take it to a family member and see if they can tell what the shadow shape is!

Instead of paper and pencil, use sidewalk chalk. Or have your family member stand outside on the sidewalk. Draw around that person's shadow. Can you tell who it is?

Instead of tracing the shape, add additional drawings to the shadow: crowns, conversation balloons, balls, etc.

We can't SEE God. But we can see what he does. It is like seeing the shape of a shadow!

STRONG MOTIONS!

Don't be afraid, for I am with you. . . . I am your God. I will strengthen you and help you. I will hold you up with my victorious right hand.

Isaiah 41:10

Many cyclists use hand motions to tell cars which way they are turning. With your family, make up motions for the main words of this verse. You can even look up ASL (American Sign Language) on the Internet for some words and use those motions!

Then, practice saying the verse together while you make the motions. Do it until you are sure you can repeat the words AND do the motions.

PRAYER

Dear God, here is picture of something I want
to do. But I am waiting. Please help me to wait
and to trust you. In Jesus' name, amen.

*Even when I walk through the darkest valley, I will
not be afraid, for you are close beside me. Your
rod and your staff protect and comfort me.*

Psalm 23:4

ENCOURAGED BY GOD

ALMiGHTY POWER

EXODUS 7:1—10:29; MARK 4:35—5:43

God had told Moses to go back to Pharaoh. Moses probably
did not want to go. But he did want to obey God.

So Moses went. He told Pharaoh, "Let God's people go!"

But Pharaoh said, "NO! I will not let these people go!"

Now what? Now it was time for Moses to
prove that God meant what he said!

Moses threw down his walking stick—and it became a snake! He
showed Pharaoh what God's power could do. But Pharaoh didn't care.

Then, God told Moses to go to the Nile River. The Nile River was where everyone got their water and their fish to eat! God told Moses to touch the water with his walking stick. He did—and the water turned to blood!

Now, there was no clean water. The stinky river of blood was full of dead, stinky fish! God showed that he meant what he said.

And God gave Pharaoh time to change his mind. Another week passed. Then, Moses went back to Pharaoh. He said, "Let God's people go!" But Pharaoh got meaner! He still would not let them go!

So God showed his power through Moses again. God sent millions of frogs. They were everywhere. ICK! SQUISH! But Pharaoh still said NO!

Then God sent little gnats, buzzing and flying into everyone's mouth and eyes! Next, God sent swarms of flies. But Pharaoh still said NO!

Then, God sent troubles only to the Egyptians. The Egyptians' animals got sick. Many of them died. But nothing happened to the Israelites' animals.

And then, the Egyptians were covered in sores. But the Israelites were fine! God wanted Pharaoh to know that he knew who his people were. He could protect his people!

Moses asked Pharaoh again, and again. And Pharaoh still said NO!

So—a terrible hail storm smashed all the plants and trees. Then, huge locusts came, like big grasshoppers. And they ate everything!

Next it got dark—really dark. But only where the Egyptians lived. It was dark for three days. But it was sunny where the Israelites lived!

And Pharaoh? He still said NO! Moses had proved that God can do anything! Still, Pharaoh was saying NO! So Moses still had to wait and to trust God!

How is Jesus greater? Jesus showed everyone what God is like!

- Jesus stopped storms.

- He sent evil spirits away.

- He healed sick people.

- He fed hungry people.

- He even made dead people alive!

Jesus showed that God keeps his promises. He proved to everyone that he is God's own Son. The Bible tells us that Jesus is greater than Moses (Hebrews 3:1–6).

It's good to know God will help you show others that you belong to him. He will help you be kind, patient, and trust in him.

He will show you what to do and then he will help you do it!

YOUR TURN

For each question below, write your answer
in the word bubble of the same color.

What did Pharaoh always say when Moses
asked him to let God's people go?

Why did Moses
keep going back
to Pharaoh
even though it
was difficult?

Which of the
troubles God sent
do you think was
the scariest?

SLIME TIME

God sent many icky, sticky, buggy, and froggy plagues to Egypt because Pharaoh would not let the Israelites go. You can make your own slime by following these directions.

What You'll Need

- ½ cup corn starch

- ½ of a large package (1.55-oz.) of fruit-flavored, sugar-free gelatin

- water

What You'll Do

1. Pour cornstarch and sugar-free gelatin into a medium mixing bowl.

2. Slowly add 2 tablespoons of water to the dry ingredients.

3. Stir until a paste begins to form. It's fun to see the white powder turn a vivid color.

4. Continue to add water a little at a time, until the paste forms a ball instead of sticking to the bowl.

Tips

- Sugar-free gelatin mix won't stick to hands as much as the sugary kind. Both will work though.

- If slime is too thin, add cornstarch.
  If it is too thick, add a bit more water.

- Play with it on a plastic mat or some waxed paper.

- Store it in an airtight container in the refrigerator.

MAKE YOUR OWN ICE CREAM

God protected the Israelites from the plagues. While the Egyptians had burning sores, the Israelites were cool and clean. How do you cool down when you are hot? A great way is to eat ice cream! If you've never made ice cream in a bag, it's fun. And even if you have, it's fun to do it again. If you make more than one bag, you can share extra ice cream with others.

What You'll Need

- 2 resealable plastic freezer bags: one gallon-sized, one quart-sized
- large bowl
- ½ cup half-and-half
- ice
- ½ cup rock salt or ice cream salt
- ½ teaspoon vanilla extract
- 1 tablespoon of sugar
- gloves or hand towel (optional)

What You'll Do

1. Fill the gallon-sized bag about halfway with ice.

2. Pour in the salt.

3. Set the bag in the bowl.

4. In the quart-sized bag, pour in the half-and-half, sugar, and vanilla. Zip it shut.

5. Set the quart-sized bag into the gallon-sized bag.

6. Now move ice around so that the ice surrounds the quart-sized bag.

7. Press out the air from the gallon-sized bag, and zip it shut.

8. Now shake, move, jiggle, smoosh, and roll the bags. You want to get the cold from the ice transferred into liquid to make it ice cream.

9. After at least five minutes, check the ice cream to see if it is ready. Keep shaking and moving it until it is fully frozen.

Optional

- If your hands are freezing, wear gloves. Or lay your bag in a hand towel. Grab the ends of the towel to make a sling for your bag.

REACHING NEW HEIGHTS

It was early morning. The sun was just coming up. Jenna and her mom were ready to hike the mountain.

Jenna was excited, but she was scared, too.

"There it is, Jenna!" said Mom. She parked the car at the start of the trail head. "That's the mountain you wanted to climb. Let's pick up our packs and get going."

Jenna looked up and up, to the top of the mountain. It was so high, the top was covered by clouds.

Inside, she prayed, "Please, God. Help me to be brave." Then she picked up her pack and started walking after Mom.

At first, they walked through green woods. It was fun. Then the trail got steeper. There were no more trees. Some parts were rocky. Some places were muddy. Jenna began to feel scared again. So, she prayed. "God, help me to be brave," she said.

The sun was high in the sky when they sat down to eat their lunch. The PB&J tasted so good. Jenna asked, "How long before we reach the top?"

Mom said, "We will get there in another hour or so. And it won't take as long to get back down."

Jenna was excited. "I am going to climb this mountain, for real!" she said.

As they started walking again, it was still rocky. It was still steep. But now, Jenna knew the top was close. And soon, she was at the edge of a green and grassy place where she could see the last rock sticking up. With Mom's help, Jenna climbed up to the top of the rock. She could see every place below. She felt like a hero.

She looked up into the blue sky. "Thanks, God! You made me brave. And I made it!" she said.

YOUR TURN

Write the answers to the following questions on each mountain:

1. What is something you are afraid to do?

2. What would you like to say to God about that?

Add your own mountains to the mountain range below.
Maybe add a hiker or rock climber! Inside your mountains,
draw or write your prayer to God about your fear.

1

PRAYER

Dear God, I want people to know who you are. Thank you for helping me show others what you are like. I want the way I live to show I belong to you. In Jesus' name, amen.

2

COURAGE ROCKS

Jenna had to climb a lot of big rocks to reach the summit. Sometimes, she was scared. When things are scary, it helps us to read good words. Today, paint or draw some good words on some rocks.

What You'll Need

- smooth rocks (like river rocks)

- permanent markers or paint pens

- **optional:** acrylic paints, paintbrushes, cup of water (if you use acrylic paints)

What You'll Do

1. On the bottom of a rock, print one word. Use a word that reminds you of something that makes you afraid.

2. On the top of the rock, print or paint words from Psalm 23:4 or Isaiah 41:10.

3. Let your rocks dry.

Keep your painted rocks where you can see them. Your rocks will remind you that God is with you. He says you don't have to be afraid.

PRAYER

Dear God, I want people to know who you are. Thank you for helping me show others what you are like. I want the way I live to show I belong to you. In Jesus' name, amen.

YARN WEB

Sometimes, life decisions can be as confusing as hiking paths. The trails will crisscross like a ball of yarn. When we get confused we should pray for God to give us directions. Make your own yarn web in your room.

1. Tie the end of the yarn to something heavy, like a bed or a chair.

2. Walk around your room, unrolling the yarn as you go.

3. Loop the yarn around non-breakable objects. Avoid lamps!

4. When you are done, try to crawl through your web without touching the yarn.

Bonus Fun: The Longest Race

Get your family together to play this fun game.

1. Cut two colors of yarn into pieces at least 8 inches long.

2. Lay pieces of yarn all over the room.

3. Form two teams, one for each color of yarn. One team will pick up (red) yarn. The other team will pick up (blue) yarn.

4. Set a timer and yell, "GO!" Everyone picks up their team's color of yarn.

5. Each team works together to tie the pieces of yarn together.

6. When the timer buzzes, everyone stops.

7. Now lay the tied yarn strands side by side. Whose is the longest? Play again.

Week 6 • Day 1

God so loved the world that he gave his one and only Son. Anyone who believes in him will not die but will have eternal life.

John 3:16 (NIrV)

SAVED BY GOD

PASSOVER

EXODUS 11:1—12:32; MARK 14:34—15:41; JOHN 14:12-14

Even though God had sent many troubles to Egypt, Pharaoh kept on saying, NO!

Over and over, God sent Moses before a bad thing happened to give Pharaoh a chance to say yes. But he didn't. Not until the last bad thing.

God told Moses, "Tell Pharaoh there will be one more bad thing. It will be the worst one of all. Tell him that around midnight, every firstborn son in Egypt will die!"

Moses went to Pharaoh and told him what God had said. He added, "God will keep all the Israelites safe. Not one Israelite will die."

God had a plan for how to keep the Israelites safe. God said, "The man in charge of each family is to take a perfect one-year-old male lamb and kill it. He needs to paint some of the lamb's blood on the sides and top of the door. Roast the meat over the fire. Eat it right then. Also eat bitter herbs, and bread made without yeast. If any food is left, burn it. Be dressed and ready to leave. Tell the people to eat quickly.

The meal was called Passover because the Israelites would be "passed over" when death came to the Egyptians. The blood on the doorposts showed the angel that they were protected. The Israelites would be saved—and they'd be leaving that night.

God told the Israelites to celebrate the Passover every year. God wanted them to remember how he had saved them. Even now, people still celebrate Passover.

The Israelites did just what they were told. They painted the lamb's blood on their doorways. They roasted the meat and ate their special Passover meal. They all stayed inside and waited. They were packed and ready to leave.

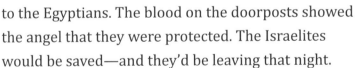

At midnight, all the firstborn sons in Egypt
died. The Egyptian people cried.

Pharaoh called Moses and Aaron to come to him right away.

"GO!" Pharaoh cried. "Get out! Leave! You and all the
Israelites!" And so, the Israelites finally got to leave Egypt.

At the Passover, God saved the Israelites. He saved
them from death. He saved them from slavery. He saved
them from living in Egypt. That was a great thing.

But what Jesus did is even greater. Jesus is called the Lamb of
God who takes away the sin of the world (John 1:29). Jesus was
like that perfect Passover lamb. Jesus gave up his life so that we
can be saved from the punishment for our sin. Jesus took the
punishment for our sin so that we can be part of God's family.
That's even greater than being saved from slavery in Egypt.

It's good to know that when God makes you part of
his family, it is forever. Jesus is with you now and
always. Your new life in Jesus never ends!

YOUR TURN

For each question below, write your answer in the word bubble of the same color.

What did the Israelites do to be safe at Passover?

What did Jesus do to save us?

Who is braver? Jesus or Moses? Why?

HOUSEHOLD HUNT

When the Israelites left Egypt, they had to find and pack up their things quickly. In this game, you'll have to find things quickly, too.

To play this game with friends or family:

1. Sit in a circle on the floor. Hand this book, open to this page, to the oldest person. This person reads one item from the list on the next page.

2. Everyone leaves the circle (or room) to find the item.

3. When you see the item, don't touch it. Remember it, and run back to the circle.

4. When everyone is back in the circle, each person takes a turn to tell what they found.

5. The person who got back to the circle first reads the next item on the list. Continue until each item has been found.

Hunt for

- Something you can hold on one finger

- Something blue

- Something made by a family member

- Something taller than you are

- Something shiny

- Something made from metal

- Something that smells good

- Something you can eat

- Something green

- Something fluffy

PRAYER

Write a prayer to thank Jesus for dying and rising to life so you can join God's family.

Use some of the words in the box to help you fill in the blanks. There are no wrong answers.

> dying good
> Lamb of God
> God's family Lord
> family love
> Savior alive

Jesus, you are_____.

Thank you for _____.

I am glad that _____.

BE A REPORTER

Did impossible things happen *only* in the Bible?
No! God still does impossible things today.

Here's a fun thing to ask another person:

"Tell me the most amazing story that you've heard about God. A story that did not happen in the Bible."

You can ask a family member. You can ask a neighbor. You can ask a friend.

Give people time to think about what you asked.
You will probably hear lots of good stories.

Then choose your favorite from the stories you heard. In the space provided, draw four major scenes. Show what happened like a comic book.

The Most Amazing Story

By: _____

JILLIAN'S FIRST CLASS

Today, Jillian went to the kids' class at church for the first time. She usually sat with her grandmother in the grown-up service. But Grandma said she should be with kids her own age.

Jillian discovered that kids' church was fun. They played games. Then a teacher talked about Jesus. He said, "Jesus came to Earth to show everyone what God is like. But Jesus also came to do something else. He was the only one who could do this."

What is it? wondered Jillian.

The teacher went on, "Jesus came to Earth to die. He died to take the punishment for sin."

Jillian raised her hand. "What is sin?" she asked.

"Good question," said the teacher. "Sin is when we do wrong things. Like telling a lie. Or hurting another person. Sin separates us from God."

Jillian was quiet. She had done those things. *Am I separated from God?* she wondered.

The teacher said, "The Bible says that God loves us so much, he sent his only Son Jesus to die in our place. It says that whoever believes in Jesus will have everlasting life."

Jillian raised her hand again. "What's everlasting life?" she asked.

The teacher smiled. "It is life with God that never ends. It is living in God's family, now and always."

Jillian thought some more. She asked, "So, the Bible says if I believe in Jesus, I can have this life with God? I do believe in Jesus. What else do I need to do?"

The teacher said, "That's great. Let's pray. You can tell Jesus that you believe in him. You can invite him to lead your life. You can thank him for giving you life with God now and always."

And Jillian did. After she prayed, she felt so glad. She was part of God's family. She can live with God now and always.

YOUR TURN

For each question below, write your answer
in the word bubble of the same color.

What does the Bible say to do if you
want to be part of God's family?

Have you joined God's
family? If you have, how
does that make you feel?

What is one thing you would tell a friend about God's family?

ALL CLEAR

When Jesus died, he saved us from the punishment for our sins. Being forgiven makes us pure. If that is confusing, this experiment should clear it up. Try this with a grown-up family member. Watch to see what happens.

What You'll Need

- water

- clear, glass cup

- red food coloring

- spoon

- bleach (about ¼ cup)

> "Come now, let's settle this," says the LORD. "Though your sins are like scarlet, I will make them as white as snow. Though they are red like crimson, I will make them as white as wool."
>
> **ISAIAH 1:18**

What You'll Do

1. Squeeze several squirts of red food coloring into the clear water. Stir it until all the water is red.

2. Now read Isaiah 1:18. What color does God say sin is?

3. Ask a grown-up to pour in the bleach, a little at a time. In between pours, stir the water.

4. Watch. What happens to the red color?

5. Now read 1 John 1:7.

6. Jesus' blood takes away our sin—even better than the bleach takes away the red color from the water.

PRAYER

Dear God, thank you for allowing me to be part of your family. Thank you for sending Jesus to take the punishment for my sin. Thank you for loving me. In Jesus' name, amen.

> If we are living in the light, as God is in the light, then we have fellowship with each other, and the blood of Jesus, his Son, cleanses us from all sin.
>
> **1 JOHN 1:7**

DRIBBLE AND SHOOT

Jesus's goal on Earth was to save the world. Your goal in this game is to send your ball "around the world" (or around your circle). Play this game with your family to learn this week's verse.

What You'll Need

- basketball

- basketball goal (a hoop, a basket, or bucket— even a trash can)

> God so loved the world that he gave his one and only Son. Anyone who believes in him will not die but will have eternal life.
>
> **JOHN 3:16 (NIrV)**

What You'll Do

1. Stand in a circle with a basketball near the basketball goal.

2. Choose a person to be first.

3. Each person takes a turn to dribble the basketball. On each bounce, the person dribbling says one word

of the Bible verse in order. (For example, "God," BOUNCE, "so," BOUNCE, "loved," BOUNCE, and so on.)

4. When the dribbler misses a word, the ball passes to the next person.

5. The next person tries to finish the verse, bouncing after every word.

6. Whoever finishes the verse shoots at the basket.

7. Play again. Can you dribble faster? Can you say the whole verse while you dribble?

8. Play the game until everyone can say the verse.

He has saved us from the kingdom of darkness. He has brought us into the kingdom of the Son he loves.

Colossians 1:13 (NIrV)

FREED BY GOD

TIME TO GO

EXODUS 12:33-42; ACTS 13:39; ROMANS 6:18-23

It was the middle of the night. But still, Pharaoh had sent for Moses and Aaron to come to him.

"Leave!" he yelled. "Take your people and go now!"

All the Egyptians were afraid. Everyone wanted the Israelites to leave.

God told the Israelites to ask the Egyptians for items of gold and silver and clothing. The Egyptians gave them whatever they wanted. They wanted the Israelites to go. And God made the Egyptians willing to give away their belongings.

So the Israelites left Egypt with lots of good
things. They would need them later.

Can you imagine? The families had always lived in Egypt.
For as long as anyone could remember, they had been
slaves. But now, they were free. It was AMAZING!

Families began walking in the dark. As the sun came up,
other families walked together—until there were about
six hundred thousand men and their families.

Behind them, thousands and thousands of animals walked. Herds
of donkeys and sheep, cows, and goats. Ducks and chickens carried
in cages—all the animals were going. It would be a long trip to
the land God promised them. They would need milk and meat.

Exactly four hundred thirty years after their
ancestors came to Egypt, they walked away.

God wanted his people to know that he cared about them. He knew exactly what hard things they had done. He knew how sad they were. And now—it was time to go home to the land God had promised to give them.

They even brought the bones of Joseph. He was their first ancestor to come to Egypt. And he had told them, "One day, God will help you. You'll go home. Take my bones with you when you leave."

No more gathering straw. No more making bricks. No more building cities and pyramids for the Egyptians. Moses was a great hero. He was leading his people out of slavery in Egypt and into freedom.

People who had been born slaves were now free to follow God. What could be greater than that?

Jesus is greater because the Bible says everyone on Earth is a slave. We all do wrong things. We can't help it. Because of that we are a slave to sin. But Jesus lived on Earth, died, and rose again so that we could be set free from sin.

How does that happen? First, we believe in Jesus. And then, we ask Jesus to forgive our sins. Finally, we ask to join God's family. Joining God's family is even greater than being freed from being slaves in Egypt.

Jesus will free anyone who asks. God wants everyone to be free from the power of darkness. He wants us all to be brought into his kingdom.

YOUR TURN

For each question below, write your answer in the word bubble of the same color.

How do you think the Israelites felt as they walked out of Egypt?

Describe how the Israelites must have felt when they were slaves.

What does God want to set us free from? Where does God want us to go?

Where are your ancestors from? How would you feel if you moved back there?

INTO THE LIGHT

The Egyptians gave the Israelites all their gold. When light hits gold, it looks shiny. Sometimes it casts little rainbows on the walls.

Try this experiment to see just how colorful it is to be in God's great light.

What You'll Need

- wide-mouthed glass container

- mirror small enough to fit into the container

- flashlight

- white wall

What You'll Do

1. Fill the glass container halfway with water. Put the mirror into the container of water.

2. Lean the mirror against the side, so that it sits at an angle.

3. Darken the room.

4. Shine the flashlight through the water onto the mirror.

5. What do you see on the wall? If you don't see colors, change the angle of the light or the mirror.

6. How many colors do you see? Count them.

When we shine light at the mirror, the mirror reflects the light through the water. The water acts like a prism. It bends the light so that we can see each color in what looks to us like white light. When are other times you see a rainbow?

SET FREE

Did you know there are still many people in the world who are slaves? Slaves are forced to work in a factory or a field or someone's house. They are not allowed to leave and go home to their families. What can a kid like you do about that?

Here's an Idea

With your family, look on the Internet. Find an organization that helps free people from slavery. Choose one of the organizations, and then select one of the following ways to raise money as a family. Donate the money to the organization you chose.

1. Everyone goes through their things to decide what is not needed. Gather them together and sell those things at a garage sale.

2. As a family, bake some goodies and then sell the goodies to friends.

3. Save your change. Set out a big jar by the front door. Every time a family member has coins, the coins go into the jar. In a few months, count the money.

PRAYER

What do you think Jesus' kingdom might look like? Draw it. While you draw, talk to God. Thank him that you can be set free from sin and be part of his kingdom.

CLEAN-UP TROUBLES

Renata loved to build things. She was making a whole town.

Just then, Mom came into her room. "Renata,
please pick up everything on the floor," said Mom.
"Remember, Uncle James is coming soon."

"Mom!" said Renata. "I have everything laid
out so I can build the rest of my town!"

Renata felt angry. *Can't Mom see that I
need to do this first?* she thought.

But then, Renata thought about what she had heard in church.
Her teacher said Jesus could set people free from doing wrong.

She thought, *OK God, help me out here. What do I do? I want
to obey mom, but I don't want to mess up my supplies.*

Suddenly, Renata had an idea. "Mom!
Do you have an egg carton?"

Mom was surprised. "Sure. Why do you need an egg carton?"

"I can obey you, and still have my piles! I'll put each little pile of supplies in a part of the egg carton. Then I can clean up—and still have my stuff ready!"

Mom left the room and came back with an egg carton. She said, "I'm glad you thought of a way to solve your problem."

Renata smiled, "Oh, when I decided to obey, God gave me a good idea!"

It was easy to clean up quickly. And when Uncle James came over, he helped Renata build the rest of her town.

"Good job on sorting out the parts you needed." said Uncle James. "That's a really smart idea."

Renata smiled. She whispered, "Thank you, God."

YOUR TURN

Draw or write your answers:

1. What do you think would have happened if Renata had not obeyed?

2. Why is it sometimes difficult to obey?

3. What should you do when you disobey?

1.

2.

3.

THE RiGHT DiReCTiON

As part of God's royal family, we are invited to his kingdom of light. Find the way that has the correct missing words for the Bible verse. When you have the right path, use those words to complete the Bible verse.

He has _____ us
from the kingdom of _____.
He _____ brought
_____ into the
_____ of the Son
he _____.

Colossians 1:13 (NIrV)

Answers on Page 221

118

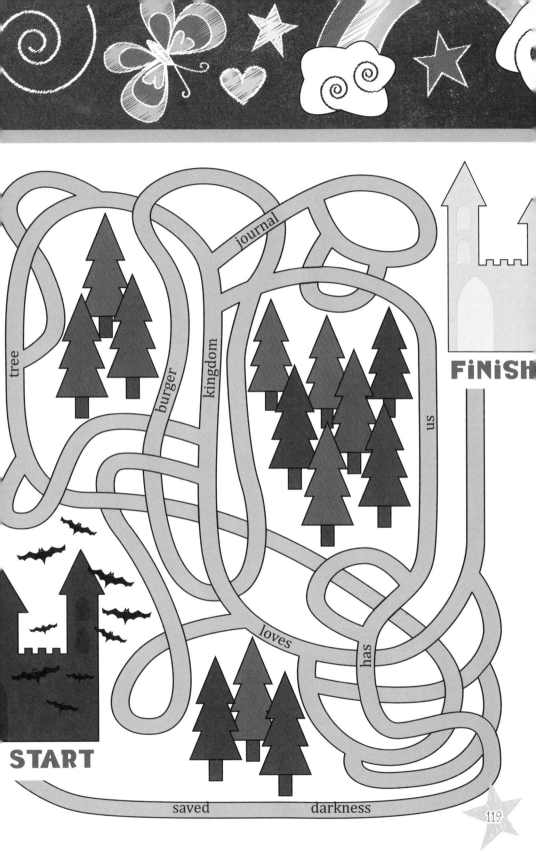

START

FINISH

tree

journal

burger

kingdom

us

loves

has

saved   darkness

119

CHAIN CHALLENGE

Slaves are sometimes chained so they won't run away. But kids in God's family are not slaves. We are free. Play a paper-chain game with family or friends to celebrate.

What You'll Need

- sheets of colored paper (all the same size, but use a different color for each person)

- scissors for each person

- tape for each person

What You'll Do

Your job is to make the longest paper chain you can—using ONLY one sheet of paper.

1. Cut your paper into strips.

2. Take one strip and tape the ends together. It's your first chain.

3. Slip your next strip through the chain. Tape the ends of the strip together. Now the chains are linked.

4. Continue this way until all your chains are linked.

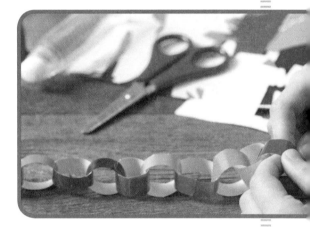

Then stretch out all the chains on the floor. Who made the longest chain? What did the winner do to make the longest chain?

PRAYER

Write a prayer to God about times it's hard for you to obey. Ask for his help.

_____

_____

_____

In Jesus' name, amen.

Jesus looked at them intently and said, "Humanly speaking, it is impossible. But not with God. Everything is possible with God."

Mark 10:27

HELPED BY GOD

ALMIGHTY WATERWORKS

EXODUS 14:5—14:31, 15:1-22; MARK 5, 10:17-27

God's people were on the move. Nothing was going to stop them. Every step took them farther from Pharaoh and Egypt—at least, that's what they thought.

Then they came to a sea. There was no way to get around the water. But of course, God had a plan. God told them, "Camp here by the sea."

So, they put up their tents and settled down. In the quiet, they heard a sound. It sounded like thunder and it was coming closer.

What was the sound? It was marching feet and pounding hooves. It was the soldiers and the horsemen of the Egyptian army. Pharaoh

had changed his mind! He and his army were trying to catch up to them. They wanted to stop them and take them back to Egypt.

The people were afraid. They were sure that Pharaoh's army would get them and take them back. "Moses," they said, "Why did you bring us out here?"

But Moses said, "Don't be afraid. God can do anything. He will take care of us."

Moses walked to the edge of the sea. All the people were watching him. Moses trusted God. He did what God told him to do. Moses held his staff in his hand. He raised it over the water.

That's when the people heard another sound—it was the sound of a big wind.

The whoosing wind blew and blew. The water began to move back. Walls of water stood up. Soon there was a dry path where the sea had been—with a huge wall of water on either side.

God's people began to walk across the bottom of the sea. They led their sheep and donkeys and camels down the dry path. It must have been amazing to see all that water standing in walls beside them.

Finally, every Israelite—and every animal—
had walked that path through the sea!

But Pharaoh's army was on the path, too. They were
behind the Israelites—and coming fast.

Then God told Moses to hold out his hand over the
water again. The wind stopped. The walls of water
fell with a huge splash! The path was gone.

The noise of the army was gone. The chariots were gone.
Pharaoh and all his soldiers were under water!

God's people were safe. The people had a celebration to praise
God. Moses made up a new song to thank God for keeping
them safe. They sang, "This is my God, and I will praise him!"
(Exodus 15:2). They danced and clapped and played music.

Moses was great because he trusted God and obeyed what God
said. When there was no way to get away from Pharaoh's army,
Moses trusted God. And God did something impossible. God

made the wind and water obey, so
he could keep the Israelites safe.
He stopped Pharaoh's army.

How is Jesus greater than
saving all those people from
the Egyptians? Jesus can do
anything. Jesus made the water

smooth when the wind had made huge waves. He healed people who had been sick for so long they thought they would never get well. He even brought dead people back to life.

Nothing is impossible for Jesus. He loves us and will always help us. And if we are part of his family, he put his Holy Spirit in us. The Holy Spirit helps us to know what Jesus wants us to do. He is with us and will help us to obey God. That's even greater than saving the Israelites from Egypt's army.

And it's good to know that God has not changed. He still can do impossible things for you, too. When you don't know what to do, ask him. When you're in trouble, ask the Holy Spirit to lead you. He will!

YOUR TURN

For each question below, write your answer in the word bubble of the same color.

What did God do? Is that something you could do?

What impossible problem did the Israelites have?

BOTTLE BALLOONS

God does things we think are impossible. But sometimes we can't see what he is doing. This experiment doesn't LOOK like anything is happening—but wait to see what happens.

What You'll Need

- one envelope baker's yeast, 2 1/4 teaspoons

- 1 clean, clear bottle with a narrow neck (water bottle, ketchup, etc.)

- 1 teaspoon sugar

- warm (almost hot) water

- balloon or rubber glove

What You'll Do

1. Pour the yeast into the bottle. Add about an inch of warm water.

2. Cover the top and gently swirl the bottle for a few seconds.

3. Add the sugar and swirl again.

4. Stretch the neck of a balloon over the top of the bottle. Tip: Your balloon may need to be blown up a few times beforehand to stretch it out.

5. Now WAIT. Watch. What is happening to the balloon? Why is this happening?

Yeast is a tiny plant. When we add the warm water and sugar, the yeast begins to grow—and give off a gas. First, the gas filled the bottle. You couldn't see it. Then, the gas moved up into the balloon and made it bigger. You could see that.

PRAYER

What is a big problem for you right now?

Draw a picture of something that helps you remember: God can do impossible things.

RAMP IT UP

God did an impossible task. He made a path for the Israelites to cross the Red Sea. Here's a challenge. Move your marbles from one side of the room to the other, without using your hands. Impossible? No, just build a ramp.

What You'll Need

- paper-towel or toilet-paper tubes

- cups

- scissors

- tape

- marbles

- paper plates with raised edges

What You'll Do

1. Line up your paper-towel or toilet-paper tubes in the order you desire.

2. Tape the tubes together.

3. Angle the tubes on furniture or tape them to the walls (with parent's permission.)

4. Place a cup at the bottom.

5. Get some marbles and have fun! Experiment. Try different things.

6. Cut out the center of a paper plate at least an inch from the edge. Make one vertical cut on the edge. When you hold it up, the edges should look like an S. Use it to add some curves to your ramp.

Ideas to Get Creative

- Cut your paper towel rolls vertically in half. This way you can see the marbles when they pass.

- Place some space between the tubes so the marbles use their momentum to get across.

- Tape two tubes to the end of one tube so that the marble can go in multiple directions.

TIME TO HUSTLE

"You'll never make the team." said Ziah's big brother, Ryan. "You're small for your age. There are other girls a lot bigger than you. And most of them have played softball longer than you."

Ziah felt like crying. But she didn't want to cry in front of Ryan. So she said, "I'm still going to try out."

She wanted to say, "The Bible says God can do anything," but she didn't want Ryan to laugh.

Ziah squeezed her eyes shut tight as Ryan walked away. She prayed, "Dear God, I am little. I am not the strongest. But you say I can do anything with your help. You know I want to be on the team. If that is what you want, please help me to make it."

The next day was the team tryouts. Ziah took her glove and her favorite ball. She ran extra hard. She threw the ball extra straight. She did her best.

At the end, Coach Tammy said, "I want Ziah for the Tigers. She has a lot of hustle!"

Ziah wanted to cry again—but this time it was because she was so happy.

God helped me, she thought. *He must want me to be on this team. He really can do anything!*

She squeezed her eyes shut tight again, just for a minute. "God," she prayed. "Thank you for helping me. I will do my best for you. Thanks for letting me be a Tiger!"

YOUR TURN

Make a poster for your room. Before you begin, use the space provided on the next page to sketch out some ideas. Then, on a sheet of poster board, write "IMPOSSIBLE." Make the letters large. Decorate your poster and the letters. Use another color to cross out the "IM" part of the word. This is to remind you of what Jesus said.

Add Jesus' words at the bottom:

Jesus looked at them intently and said, "Humanly speaking, it is impossible. But not with God. Everything is possible with God."

Mark 10:27

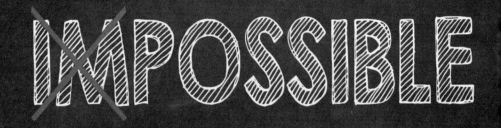

FiND AND FiLL

Everything is possible with God, even this word search. Find each word you need to fill in the blanks of the Bible verse.

C	T	C	T	C	N	X	H	H	K	O	D
L	O	O	K	E	D	I	U	V	E	A	V
P	D	J	T	L	N	S	A	I	D	X	G
G	O	D	N	C	J	E	S	U	S	X	G
O	S	V	W	S	R	J	C	D	W	S	O
Y	E	V	E	R	Y	T	H	I	N	G	P
S	P	E	A	K	I	N	G	F	W	O	P
I	M	P	O	S	S	I	B	L	E	E	G

everything   looked
God   said
impossible   speaking
Jesus

134

_____ _____

at them intently and _____,

"Humanly _____, it is

_____. But not with

_____. _____

is possible with God." Mark 10:27

Answers on Page 221

PRAYER

Dear God, thank you that nothing is too hard for you. You can do things I think are impossible. Help me remember that you can do ANYTHING! In Jesus' name, amen.

IMPOSSIBLE CAKE

Make this recipe right in the pan. Impossible? Not at all!

What You'll Need

- 9x13-inch cake pan

- fork

- 3 cups all-purpose flour

- 2 cups sugar

- 1 teaspoon salt

- 2 teaspoons baking soda

- ½ cup unsweetened cocoa powder

- ¾ cup vegetable oil

- 2 tablespoons white vinegar

- 2 teaspoons vanilla

- 2 cups cold water

- chocolate chips (12-ounce bag)

- **optional:** baking parchment

What You'll Do

1. To make cleanup easier, line pan with baking parchment, if desired. Preheat oven to 350°F.

2. In pan, mix together flour, sugar, salt, baking soda, and cocoa powder in a 9 x 13-inch ungreased cake pan.

3. Make three wells (holes) in the dry ingredients.

4. Pour vegetable oil into one well, white vinegar into the second, and vanilla into the third.

5. Pour cold water over everything, and then stir the mixture well with a fork.

6. Sprinkle with chocolate chips now, or use them for frosting (see step7).

7. Bake at 350°F for 30 to 40 minutes, or until inserted toothpick comes out clean.

8. To frost, sprinkle chocolate chips over the baked cake. When they melt, spread chocolate to cover cake. When cake is cool, sprinkle on a few more chips.

Trust in the LORD with all your heart; do not depend on your own understanding.

Proverbs 3:5

LED BY GOD

CLOUDS AND FIRE

EXODUS 13:21–22; 15:22–27; PSALM 119:105; JOHN 16:13

The Israelites needed to get going again. Soon everyone—big kids and little kids, old people and grown-ups, began walking. But even Moses did not know where they were going.

But God knew where they needed to go. He knew how to lead them. Every day, all day long, God put a huge cloud in front of the people. This cloud moved ahead of them and showed them where to go. It was so big, everyone could see it. And that cloud made shade from the hot desert sun.

At night, the desert gets cold. So, every night, God sent a gigantic pillar of fire to guide his people. The fire gave them light to see where to go—and it helped to keep them warm. When

the cloud and fire moved ahead, the people moved. When the cloud and fire stayed in one place, the people camped.

To get to the Promised Land, the Israelites had to walk through a lot of desert. There isn't much water there. They traveled on for three days. There was no water anywhere. Most of their water was gone. Everyone was hot and thirsty.

Then someone shouted, "Look! water!" The people hurried to the edge of the water. They took big drinks—but then, they spat it out!

"This water is bad! What do we do, Moses?" the people asked. "We're thirsty!"

"Lord God! What should I do?" Moses prayed.

God showed Moses a special piece of wood. He told Moses to throw the wood into the water. And Moses did. Everyone must have waited. Then slowly, someone may have leaned over and taken a sip.

"It tastes good!" they shouted. So then, everyone drank and drank. They splashed their faces. They filled their water bags. Their animals drank, too.

Moses and the people didn't need to know where they were going. God knew how to guide them. God knew how to help them.

And when they had trouble, God knew how to solve the problem. Moses and the Israelites had just one job: to trust in the Lord and obey what he said.

Moses was great because he asked God what to do over and over. He didn't try to figure it out on his own. No, he asked God. Of course, God always has the right answer.

But what's even greater than being led by a cloud and a fire? Jesus tells us that his Spirit and his Word lead us. That's why it's good to read the Bible and ask God's Spirit to guide us. Being led by a cloud and a fire is great—but having God's Spirit in us and God's Word to guide us? That's even greater.

And it's good to know that we don't have to be walking through a desert to be led by God's Spirit. But like the Israelites, we don't have to know exactly where we are going because we know who is leading us. Jesus gave us his Spirit and his Word so that all of God's family can know what to do. All we need to do is ask, listen, and obey.

YOUR TURN

For each question below, write your answer in the word bubble of the same color.

How did God guide the Israelites?

How did God make the bad water good?

Who guides you in your life? Who gives you advice?

Who and what does Jesus give us to guide us?

ANiMAL CODe

When the Israelites traveled, they brought all their animals with them. Imagine trying to feed your family and your pets in the desert. It wasn't easy. The Israelites had to trust God to take care of them.

The verse for this activity is all about trust. Break the code below using the first letter of each animal's name to complete Proverbs 3:5. Some of the letters have been filled in for you.

PRAYeR

Dear God, lots of times, I think I know what to do. Please stop me from taking action too fast. Help me to ask you what to do EVERY time I need help. Thank you. In Jesus' name, amen.

Answers on Page 221

_____ _____ **u** _____ _____ in the _____ _____ _____ _____

with _____ _____ _____ your _____ _____ _____ _____ _____;

do not _____ _____ _____ _____ **N** _____

on your _____ _____ **N** understanding.

Proverbs 3:5

143

SAY IT WiTH SiGNS

There were no signs in the desert for the Israelites to follow. So they followed God. Make some signs for your room.

- Make a sign for your door. Use funky letters and your favorite colors.

- Make a doorknocker. Say, "Welcome" on one side and "Busy" on the other.

- Name your mirror. Put a poem beside your mirror that reminds you how beautiful you are.

Be sure to check with your parents before putting anything up on your walls. They may want you to use something like Sticky Tack so you don't ruin your walls.

Bonus Road Hunt

This is a simple game to play with your family while you're on the road. Make a list of all the common road signs:

Stop	School Zone	No bikes
Exit	No Passing	Speed Limit
No Turn on Red	No U Turn	Dead End
Right Arrow	Hidden Drive	Parking
Left Arrow	Watch for Pedestrians	Railroad Crossing
Rest Stop	Slow Children	Yield
Construction	Deaf Child	Animal Crossing
Speedbump ahead	One Way	Bridge
Falling Rocks	Wrong Way	Gas
		Traffic Lights

Beside each road sign, make a tally mark to keep score of how many you see.

Add bonus places for fun

Fast-food restaurant that serves tacos	Barn	Forest or cacti
Coffee shop	Silo	Building taller than three stories
	Lake or pond	Historical monument

TEST TROUBLES

Phoebe stared at the paper in front of her. Her teacher, Ms. Jackson, announced to the class, "Read the words. Then answer the questions. You have ten minutes."

The big test had a lot of words. The letters were hard to read. Phoebe looked and looked. The letters looked like they were under water.

She could not understand the words. She set her pencil down. *I can't do this*, she said to herself.

Then she remembered something her dad often said. "If you don't know what to do, ask God. He will tell you what you need to know."

Phoebe looked at the clock. The time was going fast. She took a deep breath. "God," she prayed, "I can't read these words. What do I need to know? Please lead me."

Phoebe looked out the window for a little bit. Then she looked back at the test. Wow! Now, her eyes seemed to work OK. She could see all the words. She began to read. Then she answered the questions. She wrote the last answer just when Ms. Jackson said, "Ten minutes. Time is up."

Phoebe was amazed. God had helped her and showed her what to do so that she could see the words.

That night at dinner, Phoebe told her mom about the test. Mom said, "I am going to call the eye doctor to get you an appointment. Maybe there is something we can do to help you see better."

"That's good!" said Phoebe. "But I'm sure glad God helped me know what to do in the test, even without glasses!"

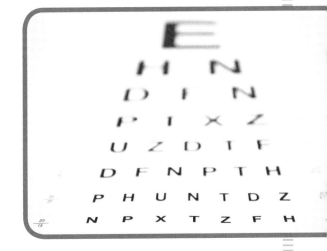

YOUR TURN

Draw or write your answers:

1. What is something that is easy for you to do?

2. What is something that is hard for you?

3. Can you think of a time when you should have prayed, but didn't?

1.

2.

3.

DO YOU DRAW WHAT I DRAW?

Everyone sees the world differently. How we view the world, affects our imaginations. Two people can hear the same description and have different ideas in their heads. Do this activity with your friends or family to see for yourself.

1. One person reads the directions aloud.

2. Everyone draws as the directions are read.

3. After all directions are read and everyone has drawn, show each other your papers.

Directions

1. Draw a circle in the middle of the page.

2. Draw some wiggly lines.

3. Draw a circle smaller than the first one.

4. Draw three triangles near the corner of the page.

5. Draw a straight line.

6. Draw two squares near the circle.

7. Draw the biggest triangle you can.

8. Draw a cat in the triangle.

9. Draw a tree.

10. Draw a sun.

Are they all the same? No—but you all followed the directions!

PRAYER

Dear God, thank you for always listening when I pray. Sometimes I am not good at listening, but I want your advice. What do I need to know? What do I need to do? In Jesus' name, amen.

James 1:5 says God will give us wisdom when we ask. Draw or write ideas that come to your mind as you read and think about this verse.

TRUST ME TO GUIDE

It's hard to trust your sight when you can't see correctly. It's even harder when you can't see at all. In those moments, you have to put your trust in someone else. Play this game to test your trust.

What You'll Need

- blindfold

- simple items for an obstacle course (chairs, boxes, pillows, etc.)

What You'll Do

1. Set up a simple obstacle course. Set chairs around, put out a box to step over—make it simple so everyone in your family can play.

2. Choose one person to wear the blindfold.

3. Choose someone to be the guide.

4. For the first round, the guide walks beside the blindfolded person. They hold the blindfolded person's hand and tell them where to go.

5. For the second round, the guide uses only their voice to guide the blindfolded person. The guide may walk near the person, but will not use their hands to guide them.

After you've played at least twice, talk about:

- What does it feel like to be guided?

- Was it harder to be blindfolded or to be the guide? Why?

- What are some ways God guides us?

Put God's kingdom first. Do what he wants you to do.
Then all those things will also be given to you.

Matthew 6:33 (NIRV)

ASKING GOD

CLOUDY WITH A CHANCE OF MANNA

EXODUS 16:1—17:7; MATTHEW 6:25-33

Day after day after day, God's people walked across the hot sand. The food they brought was almost gone.

There was no store. No fields. No trees.

"What shall we eat?" the people asked Moses.

Moses didn't have any answers. But Moses knew who did have the answers. Moses prayed to God. God told Moses, "I will send food."

That night, God sent flocks of small birds to the people's camp. God sent plenty of meat to eat. But God gave them even more.

The next morning the ground was covered with little white flakes. "What is it?" the people asked.

"This is the bread God sent," Moses said.

The people picked up the bread and tasted it. Wow. It tasted good. They called the bread *manna*. Manna means "What is it?"

For forty years, God sent manna every day. The Israelites always had food. God took care of his people.
But imagine how much water this huge group of people and animals needed every day. Now they were low on water again. That made them complain.

"Are we going to die of thirst?" they asked Moses. "We need water. Give us water, Moses!"

"You keep complaining," Moses said. "It's time that you believe God will take care of you!"

The people kept grumbling.

God told Moses what to do.

God led Moses and the leaders of the Israelites to a special place in the desert. A very big rock was sitting there. Moses lifted his walking stick, and then swung it hard against the rock.

The moment Moses' walking stick hit the rock, water gushed out. There was enough water for everyone. Everyone was SO happy. They splashed and drank and filled their water pots.

God had given the people the food they needed. He had given them the water they needed. Moses was a great man because he knew God would take care of his people. He knew he could always ask God when he needed something.

That's great. But Jesus is greater. Jesus talked about the way God takes care of the plants and the birds. The birds never worry. And God always feeds them. Jesus said that we can trust God to take care of us every day, for every need. We can be like Moses. Every time there is a problem, we tell God about it and ask him for help.

Jesus said something even greater. He said to seek God first. Think about him first. Jesus said that if we think of him first, he will take care of us, in every way.

It's good to know that God will take care of us in every way. It's good to know we can ask his help anytime. That is even a greater miracle than getting water from a rock or mystery bread in the desert.

YOUR TURN

For each question below, write your answer in the word bubble of the same color.

What is something you need every day?

What's a way God takes care of something you need?

What is a problem you have never asked God for help with?

157

CUBES AND QUESTIONS

When it rains a lot, people say it's raining cats and dogs. But in this game, it's raining cubes and questions! Play this game over and over again with new questions or topics every time.

What You'll Need

- cube-shaped (square) box of any size
- scissors
- tape
- paper
- colored markers
- **optional:** decorative materials (stickers, glitter, etc.)

What You'll Do

1. Cover the cube-shaped box with paper. (Or make your own by following the template on page 160.)

2. Tape up the corners so no pieces of paper stick out.

3. Use markers to write "WHO?" "WHAT?" "WHERE?" "WHY?" "WHEN?" and "HOW?" on each of five sides of the box. Use the markers and other decorative materials to decorate blank areas of the cube.

How to Play

1. Choose a topic. It could be "ways God takes care of me," "reasons to thank God," or a topic of your own.

2. Roll the cube. The word that lands face up is part of the question. Player either answers or can ask another person to answer. For instance, player one rolled, "Where?" He or she asks, "Where do I see God take care of me?" or "Where do I see a reason to praise God?"

3. Next player rolls the cube and game continues.

Make your own cube with this template!

1. Photocopy this page.
2. Cut out shape.
3. Fold on lines.
4. Tape to secure.

FOOD FROM HEAVEN

It's not common to see food falling from the sky. But if you could send a food order up to God, what would you want? How would it be delivered? Would it be a giant order that covers your street? Or a small order delivered to your door? Draw a picture in the space provided.

Bonus Fun

God takes very good care of our needs. That includes food, housing, clothes, and more. Because he gives us a lot, we can share things with others. Today, start a food sharing project. Invite your friends and neighbors to help.

What You'll Do

1. Make a flyer. On a sheet of paper, write a big headline: "FOOD DRIVE."

    Under that, write:

    "Please put out bags of canned goods or dried food on _____(date). I will pick up the food on that day. We will donate the food to _____ (Choose a location. Ask your parents to help you choose.)"

2. Post your flyers in your neighborhood or give them to your neighbors.

3. On the day of the food drive, take a wagon and go house to house. Pick up bags of food in your wagon.

4. At the end of your pickup, go with your parents to the place you promised to give the food.

After you deliver the food, take a photo. Use the photo on your next flyer. Also, don't limit yourself to just food. One month, you could ask for clothes donations instead.

Then do toy donations the next month. If you ask people to donate on the same day every month (for instance, the first Saturday), they will get used to it.

PRAYER

Dear God, thank you for all the blessings you've given me. Help me to share what I have with others. In Jesus' name, amen.

MORE THAN A CASTLE

Arielle had TONS of pretty toy ponies and all their clothes and houses and even a couple of castles. She also had a pretty cool dog named Luna. But Arielle had decided she wanted the brand-new pony princess castle. She couldn't think about anything else.

"Dad, please, please, please, please!" Arielle begged. "My pony houses are too old and boring. This pony princess castle is the most amazing one ever. It has a water slide! I can't live another day without it!" Arielle collapsed on the couch with her hands over her face.

Dad didn't respond. Arielle peaked between her fingers. Dad still sorted the mail on the table.

Arielle jumped up, "Dad, did you hear me?"

Dad looked up, "Arielle, you have a lot of toys and other things. You have at least two other pony princess castles. Is this really something you need?"

"Yes, I need it, Dad!" said Arielle. "It is the best, newest castle ever! And Lia has one already!"

Dad smiled. "Do you remember when you wanted a puppy? You said you needed a puppy. But now you don't play with Luna very much."

Arielle said, "This is different. I need the new castle!"

Mom said, "Arielle, can you live without food?"

Arielle slouched. She knew where this was going. "No."

"Can you live without air or water?" asked Mom.

"No," said Arielle.

"So, we need those things. We need clothes and a place to live. But we don't need a new pony princess castle!"

Dad said, "Sometimes we want something a lot. So, it feels like we need it. God says he will give us what we need. But he doesn't always give us things just because we feel like we need them. It is a difference we have to learn."

Arielle said, "So God won't give me a new castle like Lia's?"

Dad laughed. "Look, God will take care of us. He gives us what we need. And he wants us to be glad for what we do have."

Mom said, "That's true. We can be thankful that we have what we need. God is good to us—even if we never have a new pony princess castle!"

YOUR TURN

Think about these questions. Then draw
a picture to answer one of them.

What is something
you are glad
you have?

What is something
you used to want,
but you don't
want it now?

What is something you really want to have?

What can you do to feel better when you don't get something you want?

SEARCHING IN THE DESERT

God's people needed food and water in the desert.
For you to get out of this desert, you need to find the
words from the Bible verse hidden in the puzzle.

_____ God's _____ first.

Do _____ he _____

_____ to do. Then _____

_____ _____ will

_____ be _____ to you.

Matthew 6:33 (NIrV)

Answers on Page 222

168

W	Z	Z	T	H	I	N	G	S	G	K	W
H	A	Y	Q	Q	U	A	L	S	O	I	J
A	K	O	G	I	V	E	N	L	P	N	D
T	G	U	B	Q	J	U	C	X	U	G	D
R	H	R	F	W	A	N	T	S	T	D	A
T	H	O	S	E	V	D	A	L	L	O	A
R	W	J	C	N	N	A	O	I	B	M	L
V	R	P	W	B	F	B	K	D	R	L	C

PRAYER

all
also
given
kingdom
put

things
those
wants
what
you

Dear God, thanks for the
good things you gave me.
Sometimes I get confused
about what I need and what
I want. Please tell me what
I need. Help me to listen.
In Jesus' name, amen.

169

FAMiLY CiRCLe BALL

The verse for this week is very famous. It has been made into songs, signs, T-shirts—you name it! It's been all over the world. Today, play an "around the world" game to memorize the verse.

Put God's kingdom first. Do what he wants you to do. Then all those things will also be given to you.

Matthew 6:33 (NIrV)

What You'll Need

- beach ball or playground ball

- this book, open to this page

What You'll Do

1. Stand in a circle (If you are only playing with two people, then stand across from each other).

2. Pass the ball around the circle. The first person should say the first word of the verse. Then, they pass the ball to the next person who says the second word.

3. Assign one person to hold the book and help players say the words of the verse. Person with the book first says the word, then the player with the ball repeats the word.

4. Play until the players don't need help from the book.

5. Can you pass the ball faster and still say each word?

6. Change it up! Instead of passing in the circle, toss the ball to each other across the circle. But keep saying the next word of the verse every time you catch and toss the ball!

It's fun. Keep doing it until every family member can say the Bible verse—easily!

"Love the Lord your God with all your heart and with all your soul. Love him with all your mind and with all your strength." And here is the second one. "Love your neighbor as you love yourself." There is no commandment more important than these.

Mark 12:30—31 (NIrV)

LOVING GOD

GREAT COMMANDMENTS
EXODUS 19:1—20:21; MATTHEW 22:34-40

Moses and the Israelites had traveled for three months. Now the cloud moved toward a huge mountain. Finally, the cloud stopped on top of the mountain called Sinai. That's where the cloud stayed. So, the people stayed, too. They set up camp all around the mountain.

After everyone was settled, Moses said, "I am going up the mountain alone." He climbed until the people could not see him anymore.

God had invited Moses to come up the mountain. He told Moses, "I have a message for you to tell the people." Moses listened. Then he went down the mountain and called the people together.

Moses told them, "God wants us to be his special people. To always be close to him, and never separated from him. He wants to give us some laws about the way he wants us to live. But first, you must choose. Do you want to be God's special people? Will you obey these commands?"

Everyone wanted to be God's special people. They shouted together, "We will do everything God says!" So Moses went back to tell God.

God said, "Then get the people ready. I'll come in a cloud to give you my commands. Tell the people not to touch the mountain unless they hear the ram's horn blow."

The people got ready. They waited. And then lightning flashed! Thunder crashed! The ram's horn blew! The mountain shook and smoked! The people backed up—they were scared!

Then Moses spoke to God. And God answered, so that everyone could hear him. He wanted them to know he was really talking to Moses. Moses went up the mountain again. God came in a cloud.

He gave Moses ten commands or laws about the best way to live. The first command was this: "Love and obey only God." Later, God wrote more commands on flat stones. Those commands are in the Bible. Many other laws came from these commands.

What God gave to Moses was a great thing. And Moses was a great hero for obeying God and going up that mountain. But Jesus did something even greater.

Someone once asked Jesus, "What's the greatest command?"

> Jesus said, "Love the Lord your God with all your heart and with all your soul. Love him with all your mind and with all your strength." And here is the second one. "Love your neighbor as you love yourself." There is no commandment more important than these."

God gave Moses ten commands. They are often called the Ten Commandments.

Jesus gave just two commands. Those two are so important that all others come from them. Jesus' commands are simple: First, love God and then, love others. So when we obey Jesus' two commands, we are obeying all ten commands God gave to Moses.

God wants us to be his special people, too. But we don't do that by obeying his commands perfectly. You see, Jesus obeyed God perfectly. And he took the punishment we deserved for not always obeying. When we believe in Jesus, he makes us right with God. Then, we can be his special people, close to God forever.

We are never alone when we try to obey God. We can ask God to help us love him and love others with everything we have. He will help us. God loves us.

YOUR TURN

For each question below, write your answer
in the word bubble of the same color.

What was the first command God told Moses?

What are ways we
can show that God is
the most important
person in our lives?

What are ways
we show we love
other people?

175

BOLD PRINTS

Moses chiseled God's commands into stone tablets. You can make your own tablets with Styrofoam stamps. Write words of encouragement or create cool designs.

What You'll Need

- watercolor markers
- pencil
- styrofoam plates or trays
- scissors
- paper
- **optional:** paintbrush, cup of water

What You'll Do

1. Cut a 3-inch square from the Styrofoam.

2. Use the pencil to make a design. Make deep grooves.

3. Use the markers to color the whole stamp. Leave the grooves blank.

4. Turn your colored square over onto the paper. Press it down.

5. Lift to see your print!

6. If the color isn't bold, lightly paint a little water over the paper before you make another print. It should make the color brighter.

PRAYER

Dear God, here, I'm drawing the face of someone who is easy to love.

The person I'm drawing below is not easy to love. Please help me love this person. Thank you for loving me. In Jesus' name, amen.

COMMANDMENT CHARADES

When Moses came down from the mountain all the Israelites had to learn God's rules. This is a fun way to learn the Ten Commandments.

What You'll Do

1. Each player silently chooses one commandment to act out.

2. Take turns to act out each one.

3. Leave these pages open so that the commandments are easy to see.

4. When you have acted out every command, then close the book.

5. Now play again. See if you can guess which command is being acted out.

Ten Commands God Gave Moses

1. Worship only God.

2. Don't have idols (images of fake gods).

3. Respect God's name.

4. Rest one day a week to honor God.

5. Respect your parents.

6. Don't kill.

7. Be faithful to your wife or husband.

8. Don't take what is not yours.

9. Don't lie.

10. Be glad for what you have.

NEW FRIENDS

It was Sasha's first day of school. Sasha was very glad that she could hear well with her hearing aids. But people at her old school often said mean things to her about her hearing aids. When she wore them, she could hear them say mean things. If she didn't wear them, everything was quiet. She hoped people would be nicer at this school.

Sasha hung her lunchbox in her cubby. Then she saw some girls whispering and staring at her. They were blocking the doorway of the classroom. Sasha was scared to go into the classroom. So she stood outside the door.

She prayed, "God, help me. Please let someone in there be kind and not mean."

The girls went into the classroom. Sasha followed after a few seconds. Then Miss Bing saw her. She smiled at Sasha and came to the door.

"Hello!" she said. "You must be Sasha! Welcome to our class."

She brought Sasha into the room. Some people stared at her hearing aids. But two people looked at her and smiled.

"Those are the people I want to be my friends," she thought.

Komal gave her an extra-big smile. She pointed at her own ears. She had hearing aids, too! That made Sasha smile big. She waved at Komal.

Komal told Miss Bing, "I want to be Sasha's class buddy! We have a lot to talk about!"

Sasha smiled. Inside, she prayed, "Thanks, God, for giving me a friend who is kind. She even has hearing aids!"

YOUR TURN

Think about these questions. Then draw pictures to answer two of them.

Who is someone you know who has a physical or learning challenge?

What makes you feel like you're different from other kids?

What are three ways you can show love and kindness to a person who is different from you?

COLOR CODES

Have you ever missed information because you weren't listening? If you only hear part of the sentence, it doesn't make any sense! The verse today is missing all the vowels. It doesn't make any sense.

- Use the color key.

- Write the correct letters in the colored boxes.

- Discover the meaning.

Color Key

A

E

I

O

U

Can you close your eyes and still say the verse? Try it!

"Love the Lord your God with all your heart and with all your soul. Love him with all your mind and with all your strength."

And here is the second one. "Love your neighbor as you love yourself."

There is no commandment more important than these.

Mark 12:30-31 (NIRV)

LOVE YOUR NEIGHBOR

It's scary to be the new person at school. Nobody likes to feel left out. Try one of these simple ways your family can show love to your neighbors.

1. Ask your parents to help you find someone who needs help with yardwork, housework. Have them set up a time when you will go with them to that person's house and do the work that needs to be done. Before you go, make a list together of the tools and items you'll need.

2. Bake goodies and serve your neighbors. Make enough cookies or cupcakes to share. Deliver them with your parents. If you don't know your neighbors well, take time to talk with them, too!

3. Have a party in your front yard and invite your neighbors. It can be simple: offer ice cream, cookies, and drinks. Set out lawn chairs so that people can talk with each other. You can play simple "get to know you" games such as lining up by birthday (not the year, but the month and day), or by the first letter of each person's first name.

PRAYER

Dear God, thank you for helping me show kindness to kids who are not like me. Thank you for helping me be kind to people who are not kind to me. In Jesus' name, amen.

God is faithful and fair. If we confess our sins, he will forgive our sins. He will forgive every wrong thing we have done. He will make us pure.

1 John 1:9 (NIrV)

CONFESSING TO GOD

DESTROYING IDOLS

(EXODUS 32:1–12; ROMANS 5:8,18–19)

Moses and his helper, Joshua, climbed up Mount Sinai again. Joshua stopped partway up and waited while Moses went to the top. Moses spent time with God at the top of the mountain. God talked with Moses. God also wrote on flat stones the commands he wanted his people to remember.

Weeks went by. Where was Moses? Was he dead? The Israelites were tired of waiting for their leader. They told Moses' brother, Aaron, "Make us an idol to lead us. We don't know what happened to Moses."

Already they had forgotten that they wanted to be God's special people. They had already forgotten God's first rule: Worship only the one true God.

Aaron said, "Give me all your gold earrings." Everyone gave Aaron their gold. He melted the gold and shaped it to look like a calf. He said, "This is your god, who brought you up out of Egypt!"

What? No golden baby cow brought them out of Egypt.

But, the next morning people brought offerings to give to the idol. They danced and sang before the golden calf.

Moses had been on the mountain with God for forty days. Moses didn't know what the Israelites were doing, but God knew. God told Moses, "Go down. These people are worshiping an idol. They do not want to obey me!"

God was so angry. He could have gotten rid of all the people and started over with Moses. But he didn't. He had mercy on these people who had disobeyed him.

Moses hurried down the mountain with Joshua. Moses carried the stone tablets where God had written his commands. They could see people dancing and bowing to this idol,  this false god. Moses was so angry, he threw down the stone tablets. They shattered into pieces.

Then Moses grabbed the idol and threw it into the fire. He called out, "Who is on the Lord's side? Join me here!" Some people stood by Moses, but many others refused to obey God.

Moses knew the people needed to ask God to forgive them for their terrible sin. The next day he said, "You have sinned a great sin, but I will ask God to forgive you." Moses went back up the mountain. He told God, "Please forgive them. If not, take my name out of your book of life. I will take their sin." Moses showed great love for his people. He was willing to be punished for their wrong—and he had not done anything wrong.

The people had not kept their promise to be God's special people. They had disobeyed God's command to worship only him. God punished the people. But later, God showed them that he did forgive them. That was great forgiveness. God forgave the Israelites because he loved them.

God loves everyone else, too. That is why he sent Jesus. Jesus was willing to be punished for all the wrong things people do. He did that so that we can be forgiven of all our sin. Forever! That's even greater than Moses being willing to die for his people. Jesus died for all our sin, so that we all can be close to God.

It's good to know that when we do wrong things, God will forgive us. God's Word says that if we tell the truth about what we have done and ask God to forgive us, he will. He wants us to turn away from sin and be close to him.

YOUR TURN

For each question below, write your answer in the word bubbles of the same color.

What law did the people break?

Why did the Israelites want Aaron to make them an idol?

What did Jesus do so that everyone can be forgiven of sin?

AROUND THE CIRCLE

The Israelites made a golden idol when Moses was gone. Idols are dangerous because they take our focus away from God. Idols can be anything—food, video games, clothes, popularity. They trap us in a cycle away from God. To break out, we need to turn back to God and confess our sins.

This puzzle will send you around and back. Start at the *T* at the top. Go around the circle clockwise (to the right), but skip every other letter. The first three letters have been done for you. Write each letter in order as you go. When you come to the blue arrow, turn around and skip every other letter again. Each letter in order gives you the secret message.

T O C _ _ _ _ _ _

_ _ _ _ _ _ _ _ _

_ _ _ _ _ _

_ _ _ _ _ _ _ _ _ _

_ _ _ .

Answers on Page 222

START

PRAYER

Draw something in the circle that reminds you of God's forgiveness.
While you draw, tell God the truth about things you have done.
Ask God to forgive you. Then thank him for forgiving you.

NO MISTAKES ART

No mistake is too great for God to forgive. When you do something wrong, confess it. He will forgive you. In this art activity, there is no way to make a mistake. Just have fun.

What You'll Need

- oil pastels (or crayons, but oil pastels are preferred)

- white paper (at least two sheets)

- pencil

What You'll Do

1. Use the pastels or crayons to color heavily on a sheet of paper. Use lots of different colors. Experiment with mixing the colors where they come together.

2. Press hard so that you make the color thick.

3. Now lay a second sheet of paper over the colored paper.

4. Use the pencil to make a design on the second sheet. Make circles, straight lines, squiggles, anything you like.

5. Fill in the entire page with pencil designs.

6. Don't worry about making a mistake. Make your "mistake" part of your design.

7. When you're finished with making designs, remove the top paper. Look at the back to discover the colorful, cool designs you made.

Optional

Fold a sheet of paper in half. Color on one half, and then fold over the blank half and make your pencil designs. This is better for people whose hands get tired.

PRAYER

Dear God, I do things wrong sometimes. Please help me to say what is true, even when I think I will get in trouble. Please help me remember that you will forgive me. Thank you for loving me. In Jesus' name, amen.

SMASHED

Sofia's big sister, Kennedy, had just gotten a new phone. She had babysat for months to earn money for the phone but never had enough. But today was Kennedy's birthday. And their mom had given Kennedy the rest of the money she needed to buy the phone. This was the best phone ever. It could do all kinds of cool things.

Of course, Sofia wanted to see the phone. She did not have a phone at all!

But Kennedy was in high school. She even had her own car. And she had left her new phone at home to charge it.

Sofia saw the phone lying on the table. *Kennedy won't know if I use the phone.* She thought.

Sofia took the phone off the charger. She decided to try the camera. She took some selfies. *I'll delete those later so Kennedy will never know.*

Then Sofia took the phone outside to see how the zoom on the camera would work. *This is really cool.* She thought. She took a picture of the house.

Just then, Mom called, "Sofia! Where are you? I need you to come now!"

Oh, no! What can I do with the phone? She wondered. *I can't take it in. If Mom knows I have it, I'll be in trouble!*

So Sofia set the phone down on the driveway. Then she ran into the house. When Sofia got into the house, she heard Kennedy's car pull up.

Crunch. Kennedy's car ran right over her new phone! Sofia ran outside. The phone was all smashed.

Kennedy got out of her car. "How did my new phone get on the driveway?" she yelled.

Sofia's face turned red— there no way out of this trouble. Sofia just stood there. Mom came outside, too. She looked at the smashed phone in Kennedy's hand.

"Whoever did this is going to pay! " Kennedy cried.

"Sofia, what do you know about this?" Mom asked.

Sofia looked at the ground. She said to God, "I did wrong. Please forgive me. Help me!"

Sofia took a deep breath. Then she said, "I saw the phone on the charger. I came outside to take pictures with it. Then, Mom called me and I got scared. I left it in the driveway."

Kennedy smacked her hand to her forehead. "Why me?" she asked, "It took me months to save up for this phone!"

Sofia piped up, "I will give you all the money I saved for my new bike. It was my fault. I'm sorry."

Kennedy walked away. She was still very angry. She went into the house.

Sofia and her mom walked into the house, feeling awful. What a sad way to end Kennedy's birthday. Sofia and Mom finished making dinner. No one talked.

When it was time for dinner, Mom called Kennedy to the table.

Kennedy didn't look angry now. She said to Sofia, "God forgives me when I do wrong. So, I forgive you."

Mom added, "We can replace the phone. But truth-telling and forgiveness are far more important than a new phone. Thank you for telling the truth, Sofia. And thank you for forgiving Sofia, Kennedy. I know that was not easy to do. That makes this birthday happy for me!"

"It makes it happy for me, too, Mom," said Kennedy.

Sofia smiled. "It really makes me happy. And it's not even my birthday! Thank you for forgiving me, Kennedy!"

YOUR TURN

For each question below, write your answer
in the word bubble of the same color.

What did Sofia tell Kennedy about her phone?

If Sofia had lied
about the phone,
what do you
think might have
happened?

If you were Sofia, what
would you do to make
up for what you did?

199

TiNY TRUTH TeLLeRS

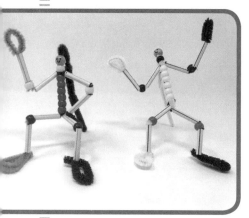

It's hard to tell the truth when you know you'll get in trouble. But God wants us to be responsible for our actions. These tiny figures are fun to make—and fun to play with. You can use them to tell a story about telling the truth and forgiving. Both are powerful.

What You'll Need

- pipe cleaners

- pony beads

- wooden beads

- plastic straws

- scissors

- ruler

- fine-tipped permanent marker

What You'll Do

1. Cut plastic straws into 1-inch sections. You'll need eight sections for each pipe-cleaner figure. Place them to the side for now.

2. For each figure: Twist three pipe cleaners together in the center two or three times.

3. Bend the left pipe-cleaner on the top and bottom. These are your figure's left arm and leg. Repeat the same motion on the right side.

4. Bend up the middle pipe-cleaner. It should cross over the twisted section of the figure. This middle pipe-cleaner will make up your head and torso.

5. Hold the leg pipe cleaners together. Slide three to six pony beads up to make a torso.

6. Separate the legs. Slide one straw section on per leg.

7. Add one pony bead to each leg. These are your figure's knees.

8. Add one straw segment to each leg. You have your legs now.

9. Bend the extra pipe-cleaner at the end of the legs to make feet.

10. Repeat steps seven to nine with the arms.

11. Hold the head pipe-cleaners together. Slide a pony bead down them. This is your figure's neck.

12. Slide on the wooden bead for the head. Draw a face on the bead with a marker.

13. For the head, use scissors to cut off the long ends. Or make them into a ponytail.

EN-COURAGE MATS

You don't have to do something wrong to need encouragement. Make an en-courage mat for yourself. Then make one for another family member to be bold in God.

What You'll Need

- 2 sheets of paper in different colors

- markers or crayons

- scissors

- tape

- **optional:** clear Con-Tact paper

What You'll Do

1. On one sheet of colored paper, draw designs, and color it brightly.

2. On the other sheet of colored paper, write words that would help a person be bold in God. Use empowering Bible verses like Proverbs 31:25, Psalm 46:1, or Luke 1:45. Or, use phrases such as, "God will help you!" or "I can do everything through Jesus" or "Be bold in God."

3. Cut one sheet of paper into strips that are less than an inch (two fingers' width) wide.

4. Fold the other paper in half "hot dog" style—lengthwise. On the folded edge, cut slits about an inch (or two fingers' width) apart. Cuts can be wavy or crooked. They should be about three and a half inches long.

5. Open the folded paper. Keep each strip face up as you weave. Weave a strip over-and-under through your slits. Push it all the way to one side.

6. Next, weave a strip under-and-over through the slits. Keep going, over-and-under with the next strip, then under-and-over with the strip after that. Keep pushing the woven strips toward the side where you started.

7. Once you've woven all your strips through, use tape to hold the strips in place.

Optional: If you want your mat to last, lay clear Con-Tact paper over it. (Ask someone to help with this.)

God can be trusted to keep his promise.

Hebrews 10:23

STICKING WITH GOD

PROMISED LAND

NUMBERS 13:1—14:38; DEUTERONOMY 31:1-8; JOHN 14:1-6

God had promised to give his people a new, good land to live in. And God never forgets his promises. Now the people had traveled for weeks. God told Moses to choose twelve men to check out the land God was going to give to them. It was not far away now.

Moses told the twelve men, "Go see the land God has promised us. Come back and tell us what you see." The men were gone for a while. When they came back, they had good news.

"God has given us a good place! It is full of good things."

They showed everyone a bunch of grapes they had brought—it was so big, they had to tie it on a walking stick so two men could carry it.

Everyone was excited. But ten of the men had bad news to tell.

They said, "The people who live there are big. They're giants! The cities have large walls around them! We're like grasshoppers beside them. We'll never be able to get in!"

Suddenly, all the people were scared. "Those people are too strong! They'll hurt us!" they whined. They had already forgotten God's promise.

But Joshua and Caleb had also gone to see the land. And the big people didn't scare them. The high walls did not make them afraid. No! They trusted that God could keep his promises. They told the people, "Stop worrying! God will help us. He will give us what he promised."

But nobody believed them.

Moses was very sad that the people didn't trust God. God had taken good care of them. He had promised to give them this land.

Once again, Moses prayed. "God because you love these people, please forgive them for not believing your promise."

"I will forgive them," said God. "But because they did not believe, all the grown-ups will not go to the beautiful land. You must wander

in the desert for forty years. By then the children will grow up. Then they can enter the Promised Land. The only adults allowed will be Joshua and Caleb because they trusted me."

Forty years later, Moses made Joshua the leader of the people. Joshua and Caleb led God's people into the land, just like God had promised. Giants ran away. Walls fell! God did just what he said he would do. Caleb and Joshua were great men—because they trusted God's promises!

What could be greater than God's promise to give the people a new land on Earth? Jesus made a promise that's even greater. Jesus promised that he is preparing a place for us—in heaven! He said that we can be with him forever in heaven.

How do we get to that place Jesus is preparing? Jesus said, "I am the way! Everyone who believes in me gets to enter." Remember John 3:16? (You learned it in week 6!) When we believe in Jesus and ask to be part of God's family, he says we can be with him forever. That's even greater than living in the best place on Earth.

It's good to know that no matter how sad, bad, or hard things may look, God always keeps his promises. We can trust him in happy times and hard times. That helps us to be brave and bold. We are kids in God's kingdom—and he is the king who can do anything!

YOUR TURN

For each question below, write your answer
in the word bubble of the same color.

Why were the Israelites scared of the Promised Land?

What were the names
of the two men who
believed God would
protect them?

What promise
did Jesus make to
God's family?

SPINNER STORIES

Twelve Israelites saw the Promised Land, but they did not see the same thing. Ten saw the huge walls and got scared. Two saw the huge walls and trusted in God. All stories have different perspectives. It depends on who tells the story. In this activity, ask different people to tell a story.

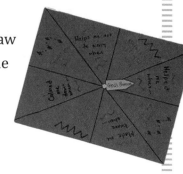

What You'll Need

- craft foam square
- cardboard the same size as the craft foam
- ruler
- fine-tipped marker
- scissors
- metal brad
- large paper clip
- tape
- paper

What You'll Do

1. Glue the craft-foam square onto the cardboard.

2. Lay the ruler horizontally across the center of the square. Draw a line. Repeat with the ruler vertically.

3. Lay the ruler diagonally across the craft-foam square from the top left corner to the bottom right corner. Draw a line. Repeat on the opposite side.

4. The foam should look like a square pie.

5. Cut an arrow shape out of paper. Write "God's promise" on the arrow. Tape the paper arrow to the paperclip.

6. Inside each section, write one of these story starters:
   - Helped me when . . .
   - Made me brave when . . .
   - Calmed me down when . . .
   - Helps me not to worry when . . .
   - Made me peaceful when . . .
   - Helped me not to give up when . . .
   - Taught me to. . .
   - Showed me how to. . .

7. In the center, use the scissor point to make a little hole.

8. Put the metal brad through the open end of the paper clip.

9. Put the metal brad through the hole and fold it over on the back side. Be sure the paper clip can spin freely.

Take the spinner board to a family gathering or to church. Invite people to tell their stories about God's promises by spinning the spinner for a story starter.

SCOUT FOR GOOD

Moses sent twelve scouts to the Promised Land. Only two came back with good news. Today, you can scout for good, too.

What You'll Need

- latex or rubber gloves

- 2 or more trash bags

What You'll Do

1. As you walk, look around. What do you see?

2. Walk to wherever you see trash and pick up every piece you spot.

3. Fill one bag with trash. Fill the other bag with things that can be recycled: cans, bottles, paper, etc.

For more fun, do this with a friend. Each of you fills two bags. Who found the most trash? Who found the most recyclables?

Bonus Fun

- Make jewelry holders with a recycled egg carton and some paint.

- Put some felt inside a can to make a glasses holder.

- Build a terrarium with plastic soda bottles. Add some dirt and leaves. Then, add animal figurines.

You can do so much with recycled things!

PRAYER

Dear God,

It makes me _____ to know that you keep your promises.

One of your promises is _____.

That promise helps me to _____.

Thank you for loving me. Thank you for keeping your promises. In Jesus' name, amen.

HORSING AROUND

Dad had promised to bring the horses back for the summer. Lily and Cody had waited a long, long time.

"I'll do it soon," Dad promised. But every time there was a problem.

But today, Lily and Cody saw Dad's truck was coming up the road. It was pulling the horse trailer!

Lily jumped at the window, "Cody, Dad got the horses! We get to ride Starburst and Snickerdoodle today!"

Cody ran to see.
He clapped his hands.
"Let's go grab our helmets and boots!"

They hurried to get their stuff. Then, they ran outside to meet Dad.

Dad got the horses out of the trailer.
Lily and Cody helped to brush them.

Then Dad got out three saddles—one for him, one for Lily, and one for Cody.

"Let's take these horses out for some exercise!" Dad said.

"Finally!" Lilly cheered. She hurried to get them
ready. Then they each mounted their steed.

They rode through the woods. They crossed
the creek at the shallow place.

They rode until it was getting dark. Lily and Cody were so happy.

While they rode, Dad told them a story from Genesis 18:9–15 . "When
Abraham was very old, God promised to give him a son. Abraham's
wife, Sarah, didn't believe God. She laughed at God. She said she was
too old to have a baby. She was wrong. She had a baby the next year.
God always keeps his promises," Dad explained. "That's one reason
I'm sticking with God for life. He always does what he says he will do."

Dad said, "It's not always easy to wait for what is promised.
For me, it wasn't easy to keep this promise! And I know
you had to wait and wait. But I did my part. You did your
part. And now we will have the horses all summer!"

"Let's gallop across the pasture," said Lily. "Starburst still has a lot
of energy. She just wants to run! Right, girl?" Lily patted Starburst's
mane. Starburst brayed in response. Everyone laughed.

"I can see Mom in the kitchen." said Cody, "She's getting dinner for us!"

"Let's go!" cried Lily and Dad. Everyone kicked their
heels. They took off and galloped home!

YOUR TURN

Think about these questions. Then draw
a picture to answer one of them.

When a person keeps a promise, we say that person is "faithful." That means the person can be trusted to do what they promised. Who is someone you know who is faithful?

When have you had to wait for a promise to come true? What happened?

When is it hard for you to trust God's promises?

PLAY RESTAURANT

Have you ever been so hungry that you couldn't wait for lunch? When people are very hungry they say, "I could eat a horse!" They don't actually want to eat a horse. It just means they want a lot of food. For today's activity, pretend you own a restaurant.

What You'll Need

- coloring tools (markers or crayons)

- white paper or colored paper

- **optional:** modeling clay

What You'll Do

1. Create a menu with your favorite foods. You can write them or draw pictures. Be sure to include meals, drinks, and desserts.

2. Take orders. Walk around your house and ask your family what they want. Or make up your own orders for your stuffed animals.

Here are some ideas for food preparation:

- Draw your food on paper.
- Cut out food from the colored paper.
- Make it out of modeling clay.
- Deliver the food to your customers!

BONUS FUN: SILLY SANDWICHES

Make some fun food together with your family!

What You'll Need

- bread (sturdy bread like multigrain works best)

- nut butter (peanut, almond, etc.)

- knives for cutting and spreading

- bananas, berries, nuts, cereal pieces (experiment!)

What You'll Do

1. Preparation: Slice the fruit. Lay out the bread.

2. Spread the nut butter on the bread.

3. Use the fruit and cereal to decorate your sandwich. Make a face! Make an animal! Make a sun or star! Try one of the sandwiches pictured.

MUSICAL REMINDER

Clip clop clip clop. That's the sound that horses make when they walk on roads. It sounds like music. Can you read music? If you can, this will be easy. Fill in the blanks to complete this week's Bible verse.

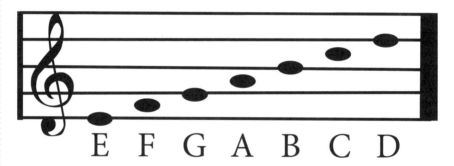

E F G A B C D

PRAYER

Dear God, sometimes it is hard to wait. Sometimes I forget that you always keep your promises. Thanks for saying what you say you will do. I am glad that I can trust you! In Jesus' name, amen.

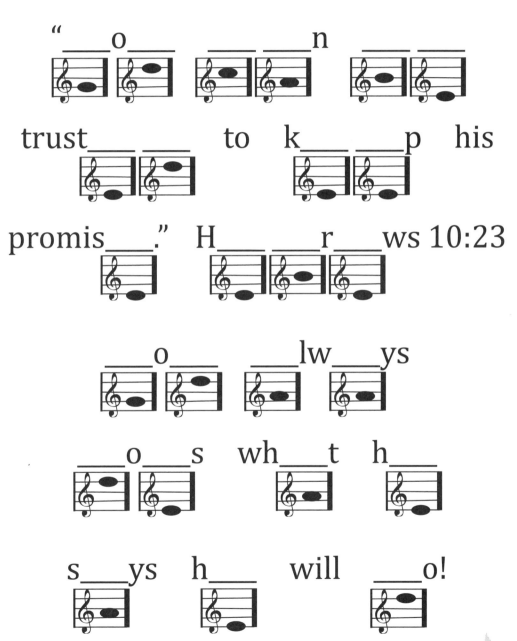

"___o___ _____n _____

trust___ ___ to k___ ___p his

promis___." H_____r___ws 10:23

___o___ ___lw___ys

___o___s wh___t h___

s___ys h___ will ___o!

Answers on Page 222

ANSWER KEY

Pages 16–17, Get Out Gracefully

"For I know the plans I have for you," says the LORD. "They are plans . . . to give you a future and a hope." Jeremiah 29:11

Pages 46–47, Fire Maze

masterpiece; anew; Jesus; can; good; planned; us

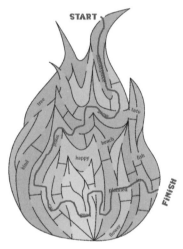

Pages 54–55, Race to the Castle

Page 64, Strong Shapes!

23

Pages 118–119, The Right Direction

"He has saved us from the kingdom of darkness. He has brought us into the kingdom of the Son he loved."
Colossians 1:13 (NIrV)

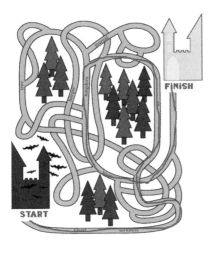

Pages 134–135, Find and Fill

Jesus looked at them intently and **said**, "Humanly **speaking**, it is **impossible**. But not with **God. Everything** is possible with God."

C	T	C	T	C	N	X	H	H	K	O	D
L	O	O	K	E	D	I	U	V	E	A	V
P	D	J	T	L	N	S	A	I	D	X	G
G	O	D	N	C	J	E	S	U	S	X	G
O	S	V	W	S	R	J	C	D	W	S	O
Y	E	V	E	R	Y	T	H	I	N	G	P
S	P	E	A	K	I	N	G	F	W	O	P
I	M	P	O	S	S	I	B	L	E	E	G

Page 143, Animal Code

"Trust in the LORD with all your heart; do not depend on your own understanding."
Proverbs 3:5-6

Pages 168–169, Searching in the Desert

"Put God's kingdom first. Do what he wants you to do. Then all those things will also be given to you." Matthew 6:33 (NIrV)

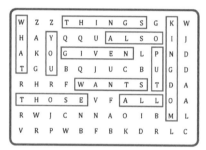

Pages 184–185, Color Codes

"'Love the Lord your God with all your heart and with all your soul. Love him with all your mind and with all your strength.' And here is the second one. 'Love your neighbor as you love yourself. There is no commandment more important than these.'" Mark 12:30–31 (NIrV).

Page 192, Around the Circle

To confess means to tell the truth about what I did.

Pages 218–219, Musical Reminder

"God can be trusted to keep his promise." Hebrews 10:23.

God always does what he says he will do!